THE MIND GAMES
HE PLAYED

THE MIND GAMES
HE PLAYED

Nya Kumari

Kumari World Llc

Houston, Texas

THE MIND GAMES HE PLAYED
Published by Kumari World, LLC
Houston, Texas
kumariworldllc@gmail.com

Nya Kumari, Publisher / Editorial Director
Yvonne Rose / Quality Press.info, Book Packager

DISCLAIMER

This work depicts actual events in the life of the author as truthfully as recollection permits. While all persons within are actual individuals, names and identifying characteristics have been changed to respect their privacy.

Books are available at special discounts for bulk purchases, sales promotions, fund raising or educational purposes at www.kumariworld.com

DEDICATION

I want to dedicate this book to
my Grandmother Mary A. Mitchell;
my Uncle Kenneth T. Dotson
& my Favorite cousin Robin "Muffin" Mitchell

CONTENTS

1

LOOKING BACKWARD, LIVING FORWARD

Ask someone about their earliest childhood memory and you'll probably get answers like, "I remember trying to blow out the candles on my birthday cake." "I went skipping down the hall with my shiny gold 2nd place trophy from a baby beauty contest." "I remember having Easter egg hunts in my grandmother's front yard."

Mine is equally vivid, but for different reasons. It starts as a sound, not a sight. There was a loud crash, louder than anything I'd ever heard before. I ran into the kitchen to see what was wrong. I was barefoot and stepped on something sharp. There was broken glass all over the floor. My momma yelled at me to stop and snatched me up as blood dripped from my foot. The kitchen window had been shattered. My daddy was standing outside screaming and yelling through the open window he'd just busted. A strange man was standing in the kitchen with Momma. He seemed to be getting the brunt of

Daddy's anger. The screaming was even louder than the broken glass. I didn't understand what was going on until years later. My momma had a boyfriend on the side. Daddy came home from work early, walked past the window, and saw them together in the kitchen.

My parents were both black and out of South Park, one of the hoods in Houston. Both were blessed with good corporate jobs. They married when I was five. I remember being the flower girl at their wedding. Because they both had good jobs, we were able to move to a much nicer area on the outskirts of Houston. Missouri City, or "Mo-City" as they call it on the streets, was the place to be in the 80s if you were black and had money. Being from the hood, my parents were used to tough times. They were also used to fighting. I got used to it, too. I didn't know any different. I figured all my friends' parents fought like mine did.

When I was nine years old, my momma woke up my sister and me in the wee hours of the morning. She said to pack up our stuff and get in the car. Then she drove us deep into the north side of Houston, which wasn't nearly as nice. She didn't even let Daddy know where we were moving, and he couldn't contact us. I didn't see my dad until the summer after 6th grade.

Mom had a boyfriend, this short guy with curly hair, who'd stay at our house with my mom, in her room, all day and all night.

One time I went to Astroworld with a friend from my old neighborhood and spent the night at her house. When Mom picked me up the next day, she told me I had to go live with my dad. I hated the thought of it because mom was quite young-spirited and would do something fun on a whim. All my dad did was go to work and go fishing.

Although Mamma could be a lot of fun, she was also totally unreliable. On my 12th birthday, she was supposed to take me to Red Lobster – my very favorite place to eat. She didn't even show up and didn't bother to call or answer her phone. Later, she said that her boyfriend had a basketball game in Louisiana, and she had to be there.

Daddy had gotten custody because Mom didn't show up in court, either. After a couple of months, my parents decided on joint custody. Mom moved to a horrible apartment on the southwest side. I'd never seen so many roaches in all my life. If I accidentally left food out, I'd come back, and the roaches would scatter from my plate. I hated it there.

Daddy was a straight-up guy. He taught me how to fish and bait my hook. He stressed the importance of being independent; knowing how to pump my own gas and change my own tire. He only had two girlfriends while I was growing up. Both of them were very motherly, nurturing, and compassionate. However, because my sister was eight years younger than I was, I ended up taking on the motherly role. I learned to cook meals and get my sister ready for school. My daddy pushed us heavily into church. They had a lot of compassion there. We had Wednesday night Bible study, choir rehearsal on Thursdays, and church twice on Sundays. When I got baptized, I invited my mom. She never showed. Again. My grandma was Catholic and didn't really want to go to a Baptist baptism. But she did anyway. Grandma was like that. She kissed and hugged me afterward. I was close to my grandmother. She always did what she could to make up for Mamma's frequent neglect. But no matter what, she still wasn't my mom. Every little girl needs a loving mom. I am well aware that it seldom goes that way.

2

COMING UNHINGED

When I was in the ninth grade, Mom and Dad got back together, much to my surprise. I figured Daddy must be crazy in love, the emphasis on the crazy part. I was half-expecting their next breakup any day. Mom lasted till my senior year. She did the same thing she'd done before. When Dad was at work, without a hint of anything to anyone, she packed up all her shit and had me and my sister do the same. We moved five minutes away.

One of my mom's rules was that I couldn't close my bedroom door, even when I changed clothes! I guess she figured I was as wild and crazy as she was. One night I was on the phone with a friend. I closed the door because I didn't want my mom to eavesdrop (as she tended to do). She came screaming down the hall and banged on my door as she threw it open.

"What the fuck are you doing? How many times have I told you not to close your door?!" I just stared at her as my jaw dropped. I was mostly embarrassed because I was still on the phone. No doubt my friend, Tasha, heard.

"Hey, sorry. I have to call you back."

Momma kept screaming at me as she started taking the door off its hinges. I remember thinking, "She's unhinged all right." I grabbed an outfit from my closet and dashed through the small opening between my mom and the half-opened door. I grabbed my purse and ran outside to my 1989 Toyota Celica. I reached in my purse for the keys and couldn't find them. So, I dug further. Still no luck. Finally, I emptied my entire purse onto the cement. As I began to sift through my shit, my mom came outside. She was holding my keys above her head.

"Are you looking for something?" She wasn't screaming, just being sarcastic and sounding like a bratty kid.

"Give me my keys!" I was the one screaming now.

"Not a chance. Maybe you'll learn a lesson or two." She went back inside the house while I picked up all my shit off the ground. I walked back into the house and Momma was standing there – no keys in her hand.

"Good luck finding 'em." She used the same juvenile voice.

I went into my room – the one without a door – and called Tasha back. She knew there was trouble because she'd overheard it. Not wasting any time, she drove over to my mom's house, picked me up, and we went back to her house. I spent the night there.

The next morning, I called Dad and he came and picked me up. He went to my mom's and got my keys back. I was surprised she gave them to him. I stayed at my dad's place until college started and my dorm room opened up.

I never again lived with anyone as horrible as my mother. Not even close. Well, whenever I stayed at Mickael's – that was pretty close.

3

WHEN I GROW UP
I WANT TO BE...

I loved to debate, even when I was young. In elementary school, if someone tried to disagree with me, I'd talk circles around them. I'd already seen my share of lawyer shows. I wasn't very interested in them, except for the lawyer part. It was like I could see myself in the courtroom, pacing back and forth in front of the jury box, making my case. And a damn good one at that.

One of my friends wanted to be a waitress, so she could always order her own food. Another wanted to be a "garbage man" because he thought it would be cool to drive around in one of those big trucks and then go through everyone's trash at the end of the run. He was sure there would be valuable stuff people had accidentally thrown away.

I carried my goal of becoming a lawyer into college. I chose Wiley College because it is the Historically Black College where the great debaters came from. That seemed perfect for me, for so many reasons. So I set out with my plan intact. Soon I found out that students in the criminal justice program got to take cool field trips, like to Angola Penitentiary, also known as the Alcatraz of the South. That's all it took for me. I was sold: the promise of a bunch of great field trips.

While going to school, I sorta designed my own field trips my sophomore year. I got a job with the state of Texas working as a correctional officer. They sent me to the Ramsey Unit. It wasn't the Alcatraz of the South. It was more like the old-fashioned, southern-style penitentiary, like the one portrayed in the movie *Life*. There were certainly some interesting parts of the job. I had to prepare for riots, patrol the visitation room on weekends, and even sometimes walk through the shower room while the guys were showering. (Let me just say that ball size is a hell of a thing and can vary greatly.) I ended up working in penitentiaries for three-and-a-half years.

Basically, I dumped the law for jails. Now I work in the emergency management field. That's a whole different bag of tricks.

9

4

LOVE AT FIRST SIGHT

It was my sophomore year in college. I moved back to Houston to go to Texas Southern University because I had just been hired at the Texas Department of Criminal Justice as a correctional officer. I was very ambitious – a full-time student with a full-time job, my own apartment, and a 1998 Chrysler Sebring with 18" chrome rims. I was living the high life, for a college student, anyway.

Shortly after I arrived back in Houston, one of my co-workers had a house party. It was in a somewhat bougie predominantly black neighborhood called Hiram Clarke. When I walked in, there were a bunch of people sitting around eating and drinking; there was a dominoes table and spades table with music playing in the background.

I socialized for a bit and was preparing to leave when one of my co-worker's friends approached me. He was 6'4", dark and slender. He asked me my name and if he could have my phone number. I could tell he was older than me, so I asked how old he was. "Twenty-four" was his response. I gave him my number, got in my car, and drove off. Later that night, he called and introduced himself. His name was Lee. He said he was single, lived alone, had an 8-year-old son, was a street pharmacist, and self-proclaimed "Man in the Streets." I guess it was curiosity, but I was intrigued. As we talked, his other phone kept ringing – nonstop. He said he had to "handle some business" but wanted to meet for lunch the next day. So, we went to a high-end seafood restaurant. After we arrived and were seated, we began talking about our childhoods. His parents were still together. I thought that was honorable, and I wondered if he could be as devoted as his father had been. Were they cut from the same cloth?

It wasn't long before I found out the answer to that question: no, not even the same fabric. About a month after we had been dating, I started having my suspicions. Something wasn't right, so I began snooping around. I checked his wallet and found out he was 28, born in 1973. I asked him about it and the lies began piling up. He insisted 28 was what he told me when we first met. Then I asked why he always came over to my apartment but we never went to his.

"Why don't you invite me over to your place sometime?"

"Well, I don't trust people around where I lay my head because of my line of work. I've been set up before." He said he had been dating this girl, and she would stay at his house when he would have to "work." One day, he came home and she had wiped him out; took his safe full of money, all his TVs, all his jewelry, and was nowhere to be found. Being gullible, I had compassion for him. So, I agreed that we could wait until he felt comfortable enough with me coming to his place. He continued to come to see me.

A couple of more months in, I kept having this uneasy feeling that something wasn't right. My intention was screaming. I followed him one night. He pulled up to his place in his Gold Ford Explorer and went inside while I sat outside watching. The neighborhood was uppity, it was an apartment complex, but as I looked around, there were Mercedes Benz's, Lexis's, and Audi's all types of high-end vehicles parked outside. About 30 minutes later, he walked out with a blonde-haired, blue-eyed white girl who was short and heavy set. I got out of my car and walked in their direction as I started yelling.

"What the fuck are you doing? Who is she?"

Lee looked startled and didn't say a word. The girl spoke for him. "I'm Amy. We've been together for five years; we live together and that's my truck; so who the hell are you?!"

I fought back tears and gave him a stare of death. Then I just turned around and walked back to my car. I drove off and bawled my eyes out the entire trip. By the time I got home I had determined that I would never see him or speak to him again. Lee called and called, but I refused to answer. I was done! He had the audacity to lie about having a whole hidden relationship behind my back.

However, something happened that month that would change my life forever. I missed my period and found out I was pregnant. I was indifferent at the time. I was just 20 years old, attending college, working full time, and couldn't imagine how I'd fit a baby into my life. I knew I didn't want Lee back. I had a decision to make.

In April of 2003, I gave birth to my son. He was 6 pounds, 9 ounces, and the most amazing person I'd ever met. It was love at first sight. He had an infectious smile. I looked into his eyes and it was like I could see into his soul. Far more than a mere baby, he was this incredible person. It was like I'd known him all my life. Like I'd known him even before my life. My love for him seemed to have no beginning and no end.

All those times I'd heard people say, "Well, just wait till you have your own child. Then you'll understand." I suddenly knew what they couldn't explain. It was beyond all of that. I knew I'd made the right decision. I knew instantly that I never wanted him to feel the neglect or abandonment I'd felt from my mother.

Lee was not in my son's life, even though I encouraged it. He never participated in any of his upbringing. I'd call to invite him to birthday parties and he wouldn't show. Christmas, the first day of school, basketball games – no daddy. He was a ghost. However, it did make me stronger. It made me hustle harder and yearn for a stand-up guy to help me raise my son.

The most amazing man in my life

Where do I end and my child begins?

I carried him within for nine months

I carry him now, wrapped in my arms, forever

I call him Lemar

I call myself blessed

He is my baby

He will always be my baby

Even when he starts kindergarten

And joins the basketball team

And graduates from high school

Goes off to college

Marries the woman of his dreams

He will always be the finest man of my dreams

God sent him to me

And it's the most wondrous gift I have ever received

Thank you, God

Thank you, through everything

5

BRUSHES WITH FAME

I had a life before I met my boyfriend, Mickael. An emotionally healthy life and some experiences I treasure. Right after I graduated from college, a friend of mine, L.E., a local Houston artist, asked me to star in one of his music videos. It was for his new song called "I Know." I played his love interest who was thinking about leaving him because the relationship was rocky. Little did I know it was a foreshadowing of things to come.

I got to be on a reality TV show. I had been a bartender in Houston for almost ten years, sort of as a side hustle. I got hired as the head bartender at a famous restaurant chain called Sweetie Pies, right when the Houston location was completed. The owner was named Ms. Robbie. She sang with the Ikettes, Ike & Tina Turner's backup singers, back in the day. While bartending there, I met and served Matthew Knowles (Beyonce's father), Jennifer from Basketball Wives, Houston Legend, Bun B, from UGK, Caesar from Black Ink (Caesar and I cha-cha danced together when I brought him his drink), the cast of Wild 'n Out, and so many more. It was exciting because, from day to day, I never knew who I was going to meet, all while serving drinks and being cute for the camera. I appeared in Season 5 for 6 episodes.

Also, I dated the brother of a well-known NBA player from Houston. He and I were together during the time that the NBA player was married to an R&B platinum recording artist. All of us would pull up to the clubs in a Mercedes-Benz Sprinter Van, and the security guards treated us like VIPs. They would escort us off the van and into the clubs, then lead us to our section. The next thing we knew, club owners would send 5 bottle girls over, carrying 2 bottles each. One time we took a trip from Houston to Las Vegas and partied hard for days. That was a really memorable experience. I felt like a star because I was hanging with the stars.

When things got tough with Mickael and I felt like some lowlife, I'd think back to times like these because they reminded me that I was "lovable, capable, and worthwhile."

6

RED FLAGS

I worked for an emergency management agency and one time they deployed me to South Carolina for Hurricane Matthew. I didn't know a soul there. I was used to that, though. I was required to attend an orientation meeting. I arrived late (probably feeling a bit passive-aggressive). I took a seat three rows back, next to an empty chair with a briefcase sitting on it. Then I saw this tall black guy with bug eyes walk up next to me, pick up the briefcase, and sit in its place. I noticed his fingers looked a bit odd. They were long, and so were his cuticles. It looked as if he had never heard of a manicure. I tried not to notice but found myself looking over at him. I had no idea, at the time, that fate had just taken a seat right next to me.

At our first break, I went outside for a cigarette. That same man was among the group of smokers, and he called me over. We made small talk. I could tell he was trying to hit on me, but I wasn't interested. I was busy noticing his bug eyes and long cuticles. Turns out, I would have been much better off if I'd kept noticing the things that were off about him. And there would be plenty of things wrong that would surface. His long cuticles would be the least of my worries.

After class was over, we talked for a bit before leaving. He wondered why he'd never seen me before. He wrote his name and number on a piece of paper and slid it over to me. As I watched him do it, I thought to myself, *I bet he's done this a hundred times before.* That was probably a fair estimation.

I went back to the hotel and found myself bored and all alone. I kept looking at the piece of paper with his number on it, thinking about texting him, thinking it would be a bad idea, and then thinking about texting him again. I became restless as I weighed my options. They both felt weighty. Like it would be a mistake if I refused to meet up with him and it would be a mistake if I did meet him. Curiosity got me to pick up my phone and text him. I had no sooner sent him my text than he responded, asking me out. We didn't have to work the next day. I couldn't help but think the day would be much more enjoyable if I had company.

So, we met up. We visited some outdoor markets and found a restaurant on the water in downtown Charleston. We sat at the bar and talked while sipping Red Stripes. Oddly, we both liked the same beer.

He talked a little about his wife, Nadia, who died from cancer three years prior. He said: "When God puts someone in your life, don't take them for granted."

That statement struck me in the heart. I thought for sure God must have put him in my path. It attracted me to him immediately. I thought, *surely he would honor me and always treat me right if we hit it off.* I no longer noticed the oversized eyeballs or long cuticles.

He told me he had four kids with three different baby mamas. (That certainly should have negated the feeling that God put us together. No such luck.) First, when he was in the Army and got deployed to Iraq, he stayed in the barracks and decided his goal was to sleep with every woman on the third floor.

He got one of those women pregnant who ended up being an alcoholic. So, he took custody of the son after he was born. Ignoring the comment about him wanting to sleep with every woman on the third floor, I was impressed that he wanted custody of his son. *Oh, he must be a good guy because he's raising his son*, I thought. Then he got one of his side women pregnant (Amber). A few months after that, he got Nadia pregnant. The fourth child was born three years after that. He continued secretly dating Amber and got her pregnant again.

I was already taking a Pollyanna view of things. Overlooking, or completely ignoring, the red flags while glomming onto anything positive or that I could interpret as positive.

Mickael had a way of presenting things in the best possible light. Even the shitty stuff. He was a master manipulator and storyteller – I would soon learn. He was also narcissistic, sure that everything about him was impressive and anything that could be interpreted as negative was someone else's fault. In addition, he was a salesman, always selling himself.

In hindsight, it's tough for me to understand how I could have ignored all the red flags that were flapping in the wind while alarm bells were going off. As C.S. Lewis once said, "You can see mistakes in arithmetic when your mind is working properly; while you are making them, you cannot see them."

I enjoyed talking to Mickael, while telling myself to take things slowly. We drove around and found a plantation called Draketon-Hall with a huge "Big House" and some little slave quarters. We took pictures by the lake. I liked it when we put our arms around each other for the photos. I felt butterflies in my stomach, but there were two species: the kind you get when you're afraid and the kind you get when you're falling in love. I drove him back to his hotel. He asked me to come up with him, but I said no. I drove off to my hotel.

Later that night, Mickael texted me and said, "I'm gonna get you, Red. I love your small waist, hips, and phat ass. I'm gonna getcha, Red!" My initial response was one of fear, again, like he was threatening me. Of course, he meant it sexually. The other kind of butterflies hit again. Over a few weeks' time, we kept in contact. He texted one day and told me they moved him to Myrtle Beach for work. He asked me to drive down and spend the weekend. He had two double beds. I insisted we sleep in separate beds, which we did.

The next morning, he got up and went to work for a couple of hours. I stayed in his room and live-streamed my church's Sunday service on my laptop. Suddenly, the door opens and this chick walks in. I had no idea who she was. She looked equally startled to see me and stammered, "Oh, uh, hi. Isn't Mickael around? I'm just here to get a spoon."

"A spoon? What the hell? This nigga! Are you shittin' me?" All of which I managed to say to myself, not out loud. She scurried out like a cockroach before I could say anything. I called Mickael and said, "What the hell is going on?!" He said she was one of his co-workers and they were sharing food.

22

"What? Are you fucking kidding me? Sharing food? That's bullshit. I'm outa here!"

I gathered up my stuff and walked out to my car. Mickael came running up, out of nowhere. "I'm sorry, I'm sorry. Don't go."

I was pissed. I got in my car and drove back to Charleston. After that, Mickael kept apologizing and said he'd make it up to me. Two weeks passed. Eventually, he drove to see me in Charleston. I had a two-bedroom suite. We went over to a quaint little bar and shot pool while listening to music. I knew I was falling for him and felt there wasn't a damn thing I could do about it. Gravity had already taken hold.

We got back to my hotel, and Mickael assumed we'd be having sex. I told him it wasn't in the cards. He said, "I'm grown. I can lay next to you without having sex." So we watched TV for a while. It was when Hilary Clinton and Donald Trump were debating. Mickael gave me a massage. It felt magical. It was like all the stress and strain just drained out of me. I couldn't imagine those talented hands could ever be used for something dangerous.

Then Mickael whispered, "Can I taste you?" I started aching for it. Any semblance of sanity disappeared as he licked on me for at least an hour. It was like nothing I'd ever

experienced. He asked if I was going to "let him get it like that."
Meaning, he didn't have a condom. I told him no! He started
back between my legs. I discovered muscles I didn't even know
I had. I started pulsating and it was like he knew when and
where I was going to move.

Mickael got up early the next morning to go buy some
condoms. When he got back, he picked me up from the bed
and set me on the floor, on all fours, in front of the full-length
mirror. He started pumping and pumping while we watched
each other climax. I was sold!

We had sex again that night. Of course. He said he wanted
to come back before I left the area to go home. He did and it
was all about sex again. And more sex. Like I just couldn't get
enough. Neither could he. I was amazed at, and so turned on
by, his stamina. He'd said he was going to help me pack. We
kept having sex instead. That man was so well-trained and
experienced at pleasing women. Another red flag. I can't say I
wasn't warned.

7

THE MIND GAMES HE PLAYED

There's a thin line between love and hate. Sometimes there's no line at all.

It was April of 2019. I was staying with Mickael at his house in New Orleans. We'd gotten along great. We were all lovey-dovey, going out to dinner, walking and holding hands, and having deep intimate conversations about our future. I was supposed to fly out that next morning, back to my place in Houston. I had scheduled an early flight. I woke Mickael up to take me to the airport, and he had a funky-ass attitude.

"Why the hell do I have to take you? Just take a damn Uber!"

I blew up. There was a TV tray sitting next to me, with a cup of water and a remote control on it. I flipped the whole thing over. Then he flipped out.

"Bitch, this ain't your house! And you damn sure can't go flipping my shit over!"

He got in my face, so I pushed him away. That's when he started choking me with both of his large, strong hands. I grabbed his shirt, then twisted it around and held on tight, hoping it would make him let go of me. He finally let my neck go and shoved me to the ground. I crawled expeditiously on all fours over to the front door, opened it a bit, and started screaming through the small crack I'd created.

"Help! Call 911! Someone call 911!"

At that moment, he grabbed me by the legs, flipped me over on my back, pulled me back in, and dragged me across the cold, hard wooden floor. A huge splinter sunk into my back, carving a long, bloody trench. I started to roll over just as my head got jerked back with some crazy force. It felt like my hair was being ripped from my skull. My eyes watered up. I reached back and grabbed Mickael's wrists, trying to free my hair from his dastardly grip.

After an intense struggle, I got away and scrambled over to my purse. I desperately dug for my phone.

Why do I have so much shit in this fucking purse? I hated myself and I hated him. I hated myself for loving him in the first place. I grabbed the phone and stabbed at the numbers.

6-1-1.

Shit. I couldn't hit the right numbers, like in a bad dream. This shit was definitely a nightmare. I started over and took careful aim, hitting 9-1-1. Just then Mickael smacked my hands and my phone flew across the room, crashing against the wall. Then he grabbed his phone. He hit, with precision: 9-1-1.

What the hell is he doing?

"My girlfriend is attacking me. Send the police! I'm at 2838 Champagne Drive."

That made no sense.

What type of bullshit is this? Sure, I'd shoved him, but it was nothing compared to what he'd done to me. I had strangulation marks all over my neck, some swelling, the reddish beginnings of bruising, bloody knees, and that long trench across my back, complete with a bloody shirt.

What the hell is he thinking? He played mind games, which often included his hands.

The cops arrived. I was taken by surprise to see two black women show up at the scene. I thought that would help my case. Like maybe one of them had dealt with a crazy motherfucker like him before. One cop pulled me aside. I turned hysterical as I tried to tell her what had happened. I was in so much shock, I couldn't blurt my words out separately or make any sense. As I struggled through my hysteria to tell her

27

what had happened, she nodded her head and took a few notes. I was sure they were going to lock his ass up. I just knew it.

Mickael was in the other room talking to the other cop. Shortly afterward, she came into the front room, told me I was under arrest, and handcuffed me.

What the fuck? Is this bitch serious?!

I started cussing out the cop, calling her every swear word in the book, from A to Z. At that point, what did I have to lose? I wasn't going to go down without at least a verbal fight. They remained calm while Mickael rubbed his head as if I'd struck him there (if I'd had a bat, I probably would have). They told me I was being booked on *battery of a dating partner* charge. Mickael was 6'3," 200 pounds. A big black-ass nigga. He hardly had any damn marks on him.

"What about all the injuries he caused me?" There was no answer. From either one of the cops.

These bitches must know him. He's probably fucked one of them before, or both of them. At the same time!!

I got booked into Orleans Parish Jail and ended up spending the night. I saw some crazy shit in there: hookers galore that had been picked up off Bourbon Street, a chick who had beaten up her mom, and another chick who got busted for shooting up heroin in the grocery store. *Why the fuck am I in this zoo?*

When it came time to see the judge, he told me that Mickael didn't want to press charges. So, the charges were dismissed. When they finally released me from that hell hole, Mickael came and picked me up. I couldn't figure out why they arrested me. Then, I couldn't figure out why Mickael dropped the charges.

After we got back to his house, he apologized for "letting" things get out of hand. He told me that he never wanted us to get that upset with one another again, and I agreed. I showered to get that funky jail smell off my body and laid next to him. The post-jail sex was loaded with so much passion and intensity. He stared into my eyes all warm and affectionately. With every other slow, deep stroke he gave me, he told me that he loved me, he was sorry, and I belonged to him. I gripped his body tight with my thighs and kissed his chest as I pulsated all over his shaft. Then we both fell asleep.

Later, it finally hit me. That wasn't his first time at that rodeo. He knew how to avoid getting himself arrested. I suspected he had beaten up previous girlfriends. He'd flip the situation, call 911, and sick the cops on the woman. Like me, they were probably super upset and came across that way with the cops. Mickael was cool and rational. It was less about sending me to jail and more about keeping himself out of jail.

Every aspect of our relationship was filled with his manipulation and lies. This was no exception.

8

WHY DIDN'T
I BREAK UP WITH HIM?

This question doesn't have an answer. I could say it's 'cause I wanted to prove to myself that Mickael and I could get it right. Or, maybe it was because I was ready to settle down and felt he was the one. Or, was it because the choking, hair-pulling, and the way I squirted with him, had me sprung? *Was I sprung??* (I'm not counting the times he choked me, in the light of day, to hurt me on purpose.)

I should've known to run. I should have known.

Well, I *did* know. Unfortunately, I didn't run for good. I kept running right back to him.

One of the biggest warning signs came when I met Amber, one of his baby mommas. After I got her phone number, I gave her a call. Neither one of us could speak fast enough to talk about all we'd endured at the hands of Mickael. So, we decided to meet for lunch.

I was sitting at the restaurant when she walked up to the table, sort of dragging her right leg. She was about 5'3, a little heavy-set, wide hips, no ass, long red hair, and eyebrows that reminded me of the McDonald's arch. She sat down and used her arms, mostly her left arm, to lift her right leg into a sitting position. I looked at her face, trying not to seem like I was staring at her right side. Immediately we started swapping more horror stories about our experiences with Mickael. We were finally talking to someone else who understood. There was no explaining this type of crazy to anyone else.

Turns out, Amber won in the horrific category. Her new boyfriend, the new dude she was with, was a member of the Omega Psi Phi fraternity. He had her take off all her clothes, put a dog collar and leash on her, and had her crawl around on the floor like a dog. After she told me that, she looked at me like she thought maybe I didn't believe her. She pulled up a photo on her phone, a picture of the pink collar and pink leash. That showed me what she was willing to put up with.

Mickael did her even worse.

He was mad at her one day and choked her so hard that she blacked out and had a stroke. (Nothing sexy about that kind of choking.) That's what had happened to her right side. She was partially paralyzed.

I know I had some crazy things happen with Mickael, but she had me beat.

I gasped when she told me. I didn't think any nasty tale about Mickael could shock me. I had some horror stories to tell, but that one....

"Unbelievable." I got plenty of unbelievable. Mickael is manipulative and very skilled at putting women right where he wants them. And keeping them there.

Did I mention the dick was amazing?

Amber still had lots of sex with him after that (she thought the dick was amazing, too). She'd already had one baby with him before all that happened. Then, after getting back with him, she ended up having another one of his babies. Unfuckingbelievable!

Luckily, eventually, her motherly instinct kicked in. Mickael had seen their two kids on occasion but was so disrespectful and nasty to them that they didn't ever want to see him again. (Kids usually have better people sense than most adults.) She didn't want them to see him again, either. So she blocked his number and vowed to never speak to him again. She lived up to her promise. He didn't care enough about being their dad to bother taking her to court for any visitation rights. He simply never saw them again.

There's no telling how many children he has out there. I know of four for sure and two possible ones. Like in a damn game of spades. I'm sure that's just the tip of the iceberg. I haven't had a baby by him, thank GOD. But I came close, three times.

Why didn't I leave him?

Why didn't I leave him?
Why did I stay?
When the chambers of my heart
Were strewn across the floor
I didn't ask for it
I didn't deserve it
I didn't want it
I wasn't afraid of him
I was afraid of living without him
Sure, love conquers all
But not bad love
Bad love doesn't conquer a damn thing
Except for conquering the soul
How can there be so many different ways
To mourn the same thing
So many tears

I can't see straight

Perpetrator or lover?

Violent or arousing?

Manipulating or sweet-talking?

A popular Tweet once read: #WhyIstayed

My response: #Ihavenofuckingclue

9

THE PAST WIFE,
IN HIGH REGARD

Mickael always spoke highly of his wife, Nadia, the one who died of breast cancer. He put her on a pedestal. As he said:

> She had this bubbly personality, like real bubbly, you know. She'd smile and had the biggest dimples. Her frame was petite. Her hair was curly. Her laughter was contagious. She looked like a little china doll. She was the cutest little thing. She seemed so innocent, you know? Like she hadn't been tainted by anything. She didn't drink. She didn't smoke. She ate right. She was always trying to protect me and look out for me. To be there for me. Until cancer took over.

He thought she was perfect. I didn't get the vibe that he got angry at her. I felt like it was me that he treated like that. I felt like it was my fault. I wondered how he would describe me to one of his "other" girlfriends. I was sure there wouldn't be such a glowing report. Quite the opposite. Like bitchy, untrustworthy, selfish, forceful, picky, and so on. I couldn't even remember all the shitty things he'd said about me.

It's like I was competing with a ghost. A perfect ghost.

Mickael did admit to having cheated on her several times, even though he was certain she never cheated on him. At least that's what he told himself. I'm not sure if that was a compliment about her character or a nod to his ego. How a catch like that wouldn't dream about stepping out on a catch like him. He was sure that she had no idea about all the women he cheated on her with. But he said she was smart. I couldn't imagine he was any less obvious around her when it came to his cheating.

One day Mickael asked me to come over and help him clean out Nadia's clothes and stuff remaining in the house. He'd kept them for years and finally felt ready to get rid of them. He was going to have a garage sale and donate the leftovers. After going through about half her closet, I went down to his coat closet. I knew there were a few of her coats in there. I grabbed one of them and put my hand in the pockets to make sure there wasn't anything left in them. Much to my surprise, shock really, there was a torn slip of notebook paper with a phone number on it. Underneath was scribbled, "Marcus, call me."

My first impulse was to run over to Mickael, hand him the slip of paper, and say, "Holy shit! Check this out! Nadia WAS cheating on you!"

But somehow I caught myself. Although part of me wanted to hurt him back for all the pain he had caused me, the better part of me did not. He was always talking her up and saying how she was so true to him. I didn't have the heart to taint his memories of her. Even more importantly, I didn't think Nadia would want me to. Wherever she was. I'd always felt some sort of bond with her and, in a strange way, keeping this a secret between the two of us seemed like the right thing to do. Instead of telling him, I checked the pockets of her other coats. I didn't expect to find anything else. However, I pulled another slip of paper out of another pocket. This one just had a phone number with the name "Tony" written above it.

Maybe somewhere out there, a guy named Marcus and another named Tony have been wondering, for years, what happened to that beautiful, petite, bright, bubbly woman they met at a bar somewhere. Maybe they were still holding out hope that one day they'd hear from her again.

They would be waiting a long time.

More red flags

> Why is it that red flags cannot be seen ahead, only aft
>
> Why is it I put myself in places I know will crumble
>
> Where the debris buries me
>
> Wreckage of the past disappears over the horizon
>
> But never really goes away
>
> Why is it that the past is never really past
>
> Life roars on while I try to pick up the pieces
>
> So many tiny pieces scattered about
>
> A red flag marks the spot

10

FOUR DAYS MISSING

Mickael and I decided to commit to each other on the third anniversary of his wife's death – November 25, 2016. At the time, it seemed so romantic. In hindsight, it seems creepy. We were in New Orleans when we wrote up a contract that talked about how we were committing to honesty and trust, dedicating our lives to each other.

About a month and a half after that, things changed. I talked to him at 7 p.m. on a Thursday. After we talked for a little while, he told me he had to go because somebody was at the door. I called him first thing the next morning because that was always our first talk of the day. The phone went straight to voicemail. It was the first time that had happened since we committed to each other. It made me nervous. Not suspicious, of course. After continuously calling, and only talking to his voicemail, I decided to drive from my home in Houston to his place in New Orleans. I got there to find that his car wasn't in the driveway. I sat there in front of his house while I called him several more times.

What could be wrong? I wondered. I was nervous as hell. So many bad-to-worst-case scenarios started spinning around in my head. I decided to call up all the hospitals to look for him. No luck. Then I called all the jails. I would have felt relieved to find out if he'd been in jail because at least I'd know he was still alive. I found his mom's number and called to tell her what was going on. She tried calling Mickael and didn't get an answer, either. She came over to check on him because she had a key to his house. She was calm, though, like this was nothing new and no big deal. Just status quo.

His mom told me not to worry and to simply go back to Houston. So I did. On the third day, Sunday, there was still no word. I was beside myself. He didn't call me until Monday night. He said he had been in jail, in a whole other parish. I believed him because I wanted to believe him. Of course, he told me, again and again, how much he loved me. I soaked it all in. Imagine being so grateful after your boyfriend tells you he's been in jail. I'm not stupid, honest.

The thin line between love and hate

Love and hate

Everyone knows they're opposites

So how is it that both

Can exist in the same heart

In the same person

At the same time

And switch back and forth

In the blink of an eye

In a heartbeat

If he has a heart

11

"THAT'S NOT MY BRA."

After seeing each other for quite some time, we would go through periods where we'd talk several times a day. Once we were on the phone for fourteen hours. Straight. We talked almost the whole time. We weren't just sitting on the phone listening to each other breathe. There was none of that. We went from conversation to conversation to conversation. We didn't get bored. How can you fake your way through a fourteen-hour conversation?

So, it was in the middle of one of those periods of long, frequent conversations that things took another turn. I thought everything was good in our world. I talked to him in the morning for a while. Then he said he was going to go take a nap and would call me later. Later came and went. No phone call. He didn't call back that evening, either. I called him around seven. No answer. I called him again. Still no answer. I sent a bunch of texts. No answer.

The next day, I called first thing in the morning. No answer. He usually got up for work by three or four o'clock in the morning. I kept calling early and later, too. He wasn't answering his phone. "What's going on?" After I called some more and he still didn't answer, I got worried. So, again, I drove the five hours to New Orleans, parked at his house, and knocked on the door. After a long pause, he opened it up, looking like shit.

"What's wrong?" He sorta slurred his speech "What the fuck are you doing here?" He rubbed his hand across his face, several times.

I knew he'd been drinking. Heavily. He'd probably been going at it all through the night. I knew he was an alcoholic, but like, with so many other things, I chose not to look at it too closely. I cut him slack, figuring he'd been depressed and was trying to drink it away. I took his hand and led him upstairs. I figured we could at least watch TV for a while. As I'm taking off my clothes at the side of the bed, I see this black bra on the floor. I picked it up, almost in disbelief (sure, I should have been believing that kind of shit by then). The bra was definitely too large, like an E cup. And it wasn't from Victoria's Secret, which is where I buy all my bras. I've had a Victoria's Secret credit card for twelve years. Little did I know it would come in handy while comparing bra labels. I could tell it had been worn and wasn't new. It hadn't been recently washed, either.

"What the fuck is this?" I was loud and furious.

"Isn't that your bra?" He didn't miss a beat.

I pulled my bra off and started waving the two of them in front of his face. "I know my own bra!"

"Maybe it's my mom's."

"Why was your mother naked in your bedroom?"

"I don't know. Well, we were washing clothes together and it must have gotten mixed up with my shit." He gave me a very straight, very direct look as if that would make me think he must be telling the truth.

"What the fuck?"

It was all bullshit. He must have been getting some ass on the side: some big tittie ass. I tried imagining who it might be. I don't know why. It didn't do me any good. I'm surprised I didn't take the bra around the neighborhood to see which princess it might fit. Big tittie princess. I gave her a name and then did my best to drop it. I wanted, so badly, to believe that it belonged to his mother.

I didn't drop Mickael though. I couldn't. I don't know why I couldn't, but I just couldn't! I thought maybe he had put a root or hex on me. That's really what I thought because how else could I explain my behavior?

I don't know if it was a root or a hex. I don't know if I was trying to prove to myself that within relationships, sometimes you have to stick it out, and I could stick it out. Just suck it up. Relationships go through roller coaster times and I shouldn't just jump off in the middle of the ride. I'd jumped off in the middle of all my other relationships. I wanted this one to be different.

12

LOVE CAN BE DEAF, DUMB, AND BLIND

It was our first Christmas after we'd started dating. We weren't together for Christmas Day, and that was a problem. I spent the holiday in Houston because he said he'd be celebrating with all his family. He didn't call much, and I just wrote it off as him being busy with his extended family. He called Christmas morning to say Merry Christmas and tell me he was going to a holiday parade that night. He wanted me to be there for New Year's, for sure. So, I gladly went to New Orleans for New Year's.

After I arrived, Mickael went upstairs for a bit. I noticed some trash on the counter. There was a receipt from Dominoes, dated December 26th, and it had the name Jalisa Mills on it. I'd never heard her name before and knew she wasn't family. My heart sank and my ire rose. Immediately. When Mickael came back down, I waved the receipt at him and said, "Who the hell is Jalisa Mills?"

Mickael stepped back a bit and said, with very little hesitation, "Oh, she's just a family friend." I also became suspicious of the white Ford Explorer that was parked right in front of his house at the curb. "Oh, it just belongs to Juvi, she left it there."

"Who?"

"Juvi. I call her that because she's ten years younger than I am."

Juvi was a chick that he met right after his wife passed away, so he said. She'd gotten a job working clerical at the VA, he'd met her there during one of his doctor visits. Her biological father was in the penitentiary because he had molested a 12-year-old girl. Mickael claimed that he could never intertwine himself in a family like that because of his own daughters. I'm sure she was just somebody he was fucking. He claimed it was over.

"She came over for Christmas because she doesn't have any family. She didn't have anywhere to go in New Orleans. I was just helping her out. I'm more like a father figure to her." (I didn't want to know just how twisted that statement could be.)

"Juvi ended up coming over Christmas night. A bunch of people got drunk and passed out. They couldn't drive, so they slept in the living room. I didn't fuck her."

Methinks thou dost protest too much.

Juvi's phone number was on the receipt so I decided to give her a call. She picked up immediately. When I told her who I was, she shot back:

"Why are you calling me?"

"Mickael's my man. We're together."

"I don't even know who you are! I don't know anything about you." She seemed very surprised and wasn't forthcoming with any information. Whatever was going on, she wasn't going to talk about it.

I said, "I don't know what you're thinking, but Mickael and I have been together for a long time."

She shot back, "Right. I know that's bullshit! You must be a lying hoe!" Then she hung up in my face.

Mickael was downstairs. Juvi called him right after she hung up on me. He came upstairs, pissed as hell. "I told you I was gonna handle this! Why do you have to go doing dumb shit like that?"

There he went, dumping blame for the whole situation right in my lap.

Her name would continue to pop up now and again. Like on Mickael's Netflix account, we were laying around about to "Netflix and Chill." He handed me the remote to find something for us to watch. That's when *Who's watching Netflix?* appeared on the TV with the name Queen Jalisa and the icon of a woman. Sometimes he could be so stupid. Or, perhaps it was simply arrogance and he figured he could just keep explaining things away. Perhaps that is due, in part, to the fact that I let a lot of bullshit slide for a long time. Way too long!

I wasn't stupid. Well, okay. Stupid in love.

DEAR DIARY, PART I

Friday, October 5, 2018

I flew from Houston and headed to Durham, North Carolina, for work. I made it here at about 6 p.m. and called Mickael later to talk. He was upset because I didn't call when I landed, but I was still upset that he was missing in action last night and we didn't speak until 3 a.m. to pray.

- I believed we were like-minded because we both loved to travel, neither one of us believed in a 9-5, and we were both entrepreneurs and loved the sense of freedom, spontaneity, and ambition.

- I believed God sent him because we were so much alike. He was like the male version of me. He's everything I had dreamed of; Tall (6'3), Dark Chocolate, Sexy, Strong, Independent, With Money (so I thought). His middle name and mine are similar – his is Jumar and mine is Kumari. And our kids' names are alike. My son is Lemar and his is AMaro. Even his deceased wife and I had similarities. Her name was Nadia and mine's Nya. I thought it was God…and no one could tell me differently.

- I love the way he speaks to me, very stern with a New Orleans twang.

Saturday, October 6, 2018

I called Mickael on my way to work. We had a good conversation that lasted a few minutes. I called again during my lunch break and we talked. Things seemed better. I called him when I got off work, and he didn't answer. Forty-five minutes later, I called him again. He answered, with an attitude, telling me not to question him. His attitude is confusing to me, especially when we had good conversations previously today.

Sunday, October 7, 2018

I woke up for work and didn't call him. I didn't call because I didn't want to get either his attitude or his voicemail. It seems like recently when I call, he either doesn't answer or has an attitude when I ask a question. It's lunchtime and he hasn't called.

I sent a text telling him he hurt my feelings and why. He texted back saying he would reply later. He didn't reply, but he called. When he called he seemed off and told me he was tired and just wanted to pray together so he could go to sleep. When I asked if he was going to reply to my message, he started yelling and screaming at me! We prayed and got off the phone angry.

- I asked him why he was being so distant. When he yelled, he was saying things like, I'm always asking bullshit, why am I always about drama, why can't I just shut the fuck up and go with the flow. He sounded annoyed with me like I irritated him to the core. I didn't feel like a solid partner, and I didn't feel like he valued me.

Monday, October 8, 2018

I was off work because I wasn't feeling well. He didn't call to check on me. That evening, I sent him a text telling him what the doctor's office told me about the pain I was feeling. He was being belligerent, not listening, just talking over me, not curious at all about my condition. I feel like he is trying to sow confusion. My feelings were so hurt that I had a panic attack on the phone. He calmed me down, and we prayed together and got off the phone.

Tuesday, October 9, 2018

I woke up trying to be the bigger person. I sent a good morning text, and it took a lot to send it. I feel like he should be the one making an effort since I'm far away. I sent the text and he took a long time to reply. He just said he was sleeping. He called during my workday, and we had a good conversation, and then another when we spoke that night. He brought up something I said when I was angry, years prior, about being attracted to one of his friends. He said he was insecure about it, and I told him he had nothing to worry about; I only said it out of anger. We got off the phone kind of late, but it wasn't a bad conversation.

He sent a long early-morning text, telling me he didn't sleep and how he had bad dreams about me not loving him. He told me he felt I wasn't being honest or completely devoted to him. I replied, telling him it wasn't true, and I do love him and don't understand why he's having those thoughts. He said he feels a disconnect from me, but he doesn't know why. I called when I got off, but he didn't answer. I didn't talk to him again until around 9:30 at night. We argued again.

Thursday, October 11, 2018

I got off work early and called Mickael, but he didn't answer. He called back two hours later and told me he had changed his mind and wasn't coming to see me. I said okay and got off the phone. I called my cousin, Muffin, crying, and told her what happened. She called Mickael and talked to him and then he called me back. We talked, and I had a panic attack. He calmed me down and told me he would come out to see me. We talked for a while before I went to bed.

Friday, October 12, 2018

I sent Mickael a text as soon as I woke up. He called and we spoke for a minute, and it felt like things were good. He sounded like he was preparing for the trip to North Carolina.

He made it to North Carolina, and we had a great time together. I picked him up from the airport, and he acted like he was happy to see me. Hugged & kissed me with passion. We drove back to where I was staying. The vibe was really good all night. We just talked, laughed, and had sex. We talked about our goals and our future together. We were making plans. I got excited because I couldn't wait for the chance to build a life with him, to have him all to myself. We had the best chemistry. It felt like we knew each other so well. He knew what I wanted to hear, and how I wanted to be touched. I saw the excitement in his eyes. He looked like he was as excited as I was to find someone to click with, someone that he could have fun with, someone as ambitious and driven as he is.

Saturday, October 13, 2018

We woke up and had breakfast at the hotel. Then, we went to a few garage sales and checked into the corporate apartment.

We laid around and watched TV. I thought we had a good day. We were supposed to go to a North Carolina A&T football game, but we just slept and had sex all day.

I saw on Mickael's phone that he had been telling people he loved them. So, I asked him why he was able to profess his love for others, but not to me. He explained who those people were and said he was too scared to love me. He was too scared to love me because he was scared to lose me, like he lost Nadia.

Sunday, October 14, 2018

We woke up and watched the church service. The message was all about "willful disobedience" and things not being God's plan for your life. The message led Mickael and me to a conversation about me not feeling loved by him because he doesn't express love to me. He went on to say he didn't trust me, and he wanted to stay in his head. We had sex and he fell asleep. I went into the other room to talk to my son, to walk him through how to mail some packages that I sold on eBay. When I finished on the phone, I came out of the room and Mickael was in the kitchen, cooking. I asked what he was making and sensed a negative attitude. From that point on, he was super distant. I went and took a long shower. When I came out, I asked why he was in the living room and he said, "for peace." He said he wasn't bothering me, so why was I bothering him? I went back to the bedroom. Then he called me into the living room and asked if I wanted to go to the fair that was in town. I told him, yes, and we got dressed.

We went to the fair and the mood felt off. I tried to enjoy myself, but his attitude was making me angry. I couldn't help but be distant. By the time we left the fair, I was completely shut down and silent. We made it to the apartment, and I went to bed. He went back to the couch. When I asked if he was coming to bed, he said he would later, that he was just watching the game, so I went to bed.

At 2:30 a.m., I woke up and he was still on the couch, knocked out. I woke him up and asked him if he was coming to bed. When he finally did, he was distant. It made me mad because I knew that the next day there would be miles and miles between us. He had no reason to be distant! It hurt my feelings and made me feel like he wasn't trying to actively be a part of our relationship. I had a panic attack, and he calmed me down. I fell asleep.

I was woken up by Mickael pulling down my panties and inserting his penis. He penetrated me several times from behind before he ejaculated inside of me. Then he fell asleep. I didn't feel violated. I thought that because I was his woman, that was my "job." I belonged to him and my body was his, whenever he wanted it.

- When we got to the fair, we walked around and found a couple of rides that looked fun. We got on one that was colorful with flashing neon lights. When we got on, it took us up high, turned us to the side, and spun us fast. I was screaming like a kid. When I looked at him, he had a straight face like he wasn't having any fun or like the excitement didn't faze him.

Monday, October 15, 2018

When I woke up and left for work, Mickael was asleep. I went to the apartment on my lunch break to see if we could talk before he left. He said he wanted our relationship to work and that he was trying. I didn't get much clarity from our talk. It felt to me like he wants what he wants, and if it doesn't go his way, he acts out; thus, the mood swings. I left and went back to work.

Mickael missed his flight, so when I got off work, he was still there. I went into the bedroom with him and asked what happened. He explained how and why he missed his flight and then got up and went out to the living room. He made me feel like I had cooties, or maybe he wasn't attracted to me. He told me he was catching a Megabus and I had to drop him off.

I took him to catch the bus. We kissed and hugged, and he fingered me in the parking lot of the bus station. I went wild. There was no way to figure out that guy. No way to figure me out, either.

13

EXHIBITIONISM

One night we were driving to a small town in Louisiana called Opelousas, where we had reservations at a small motel. We were in the middle of a conversation and it wasn't too exciting because I can't even remember what we were talking about. Suddenly Mickael pulled off Interstate 49. I thought there was something wrong with my truck. He jumps out from the driver's side and walks around to my door. He opens it up, undoes my seatbelt, yanks me out, and throws me to the ground. He turns me over, made me bend over, pulls up my dress, inserts his penis, and pumps and pumps.

It was amazing! We went at it for about 30 minutes as car after car went by. I have always enjoyed the excitement of having sex in public places. Obviously, Mickael liked it too.

Suddenly he jumps off of me and starts screaming. I had no idea what he was up to.

"Fuck! Fuck! Fuck!"

"What's wrong?"

"Ants! They're fucking fire ants. All over my leg!"

He was dancing around like a kid with his pants on fire. I started to laugh, silently, as best I could. I was glad it was dark so he couldn't tell I was laughing. He knocked off the ants and when we got back in the car, we both realized he had like a million damn ant bites. I guess he did have a reason for all that screaming. We stopped to get some alcohol pads and I rubbed some on his leg when we got to the hotel.

I went back to Houston and he went back to New Orleans. The next day, he called me up and started bitching at me because of all the ant bites. He was mad. Furious with me. Somehow it was all my fault. If we hadn't been out there fucking....

"You don't even give a shit that I got hurt. I wouldn't have gotten eaten up by those fucking ants if I wasn't fucking with you!"

A perfect example of him playing the blame game. "Mickael, that's crazy! It was your idea to go out there in the first place. If it's anybody's fault, it's the ants' fault. Go ahead. Blame the ants!"

He hates the word "crazy," which is partly why he always called me that. If anyone was on the crazy scale, he was. Sure, agreeing to be an exhibitionist while having sex with him could be considered crazy by some. I count it as being aroused.

Then there was the time in Detroit. We went out the first night there and had a good time. We were both drinking a little bit and went to a strip club. We went back to the hotel and took the elevator up to the top floor. When the elevator door opened, we were staring straight ahead, seeing ourselves in a huge mirror with a small buffet-like table placed up against it. We walked out of the elevator and Mickael decided that was the perfect spot. He pulled me in front of the table and the mirror. I put my hand down on the table. He pulled up my skirt and started humping me right there. Anybody could have come onto the floor or walked around the corner, trying to catch the elevator. That's what made it exciting. Yeah. So that was the spot right there. As we went at it, he just kept saying, "I'm watching you" as he watched my facial expressions in the mirror. We finished, I pulled down my skirt, and we just walked down the hall, acting all nonchalant. When we went to open the door to our hotel room, we kept trying to open the wrong one. We were both sorta woozy – more from the sex than the alcohol.

The most outlandish exhibitionist act – the one where the most people saw us – happened when we went to Cancun. We had a balcony that faced the beach and the ocean. We sat out there talking till the sun started going down. I was sitting in my little chair, and he was sitting in his little chair. Then, it was like a switch flipped on. The next thing I knew, I was spread out 180 degrees with Mickael's face between my legs, for about an hour. Then he stood me up, turned me around, and fucked the shit out of me. I was in a daze; the liquor, the ocean breeze, the arousal. I had completely tuned out the world. When I finally came to, I saw flashing lights from five phones recording us from down on the beach. We didn't miss a beat. Exhibitionists in our element. It was an amazing high, making a show for everyone. When we finished, the guys below started whooping and clapping. So, we did an encore performance.

14

NO DOG COLLARS. NO STROKE.
BUT CHOKING NONETHELESS.

T hings were going smoothly with Mickael. We were lying in bed next to each other watching TV. Suddenly he got up and straddled me, putting his legs on top of my arms so I couldn't move or get up.

"What the hell? What are you doing?"

"Just shut up. Shut the fuck up." He pulled out his penis (his very large 9-inch penis). He shoved it in my mouth and stuck it down my throat. He held my head with one hand and my throat with the other. I started to choke and, of course, couldn't say a word. I tried to flip around to get away, but he was holding me tight. He's a big, strong guy. He just kept at it, choking me while I was resisting as best I could.

"You're mine! You belong to me! You're mine!"

He wouldn't stop until he'd ejaculated straight down my throat. I choked again.

I broke up with Mickael after that. During the breakup, I entertained other people, trying to put myself back out there. I got on several dating sites, went out to clubs, that sort of thing. But everyone I met, all the people I went out with, there was always something missing. I couldn't get that same chemistry or vibe I'd had with Mickael. I kept going back to our chemistry and love-making (although sometimes it was hate-making). The ecstasy I'd found with Mickael overshadowed everything else. Unfortunately, it wasn't brain chemistry. It was fucking chemistry. I kept looking for it again, with other people, but couldn't find it. I hated that nothing compared.

Nothing compared to his savagery, either.

15

FIVE GAMES MICKAEL PLAYED

After reading an internet article entitled *5 Mind Games Toxic Men Play In Relationships*,* I noted it described Mickael to a tee.

1. The blame game

Everything was always my fault. No matter what I said or did, if something went wrong, Mickael blamed me. He never owned up to any of his mistakes. He was convinced he was always in the right (his narcissism shining through). "Blame is toxic behavior that gives him an ego boost because he gets the attention off of himself, so he feels better, and you feel like crap."

2. The Gaslighting Game

Gaslighting is "A form of emotional abuse where the abuser manipulates situations repeatedly to trick the victim into distrusting his or her memory and perceptions." Mickael would tell me things were one way when they were actually another.

He could be so convincing at times that I would think I was going crazy. He always talked like he was the supreme authority – on everything.

3. The guilt game

Whenever Mickael would blame me for something, I'd take it personally. I'd take it to heart because here's this guy – who I love – saying I'm making him feel bad. Then I'd feel guilty about it. If he wanted money from me, he would talk about how much he needed it for something. I'd usually feel bad for him and cave, even when I was pretty sure he was making up the reason. "When he needs something from you, something that is not so reasonable, he will guilt trip you into giving it to him. He will blackmail you with his emotions."

4. The bait and switch game

If Mickael and I were verbally fighting about something and the point he was trying to make was bogus (and it became so obvious, even he could recognize it), he managed to turn the whole argument around. To make matters worse, he'd throw a mistake of mine from the past in my face. He'd abandon the original argument he was losing and turn it into something else. "He would have some past mistakes in mind 'specifically for a time like this: a time when he screws up something, so he can turn things around by throwing your ancient mistake in your face.'"

5. The roller coaster game

I call Mickael Dr. Jekyll and Mr. Hyde for good reason. For several reasons. That guy could change moods on a dime. One minute he'd be all lovey-dovey and the next he'd be choking me, trying to drain the life from my body. "They all change their behavior in a matter of minutes without any warning, without any reason…. One day he is the best boyfriend you ever had and the next day he is a serious jackass."

* https://herway.net/5-mind-games-toxic-men-play-relationships/.

16

"NOT EVEN A FUCKING CARD!"

My birthday was coming up and I told Mickael we should go on a trip. He made sure I knew he couldn't be away too long. Every day he spent away, he couldn't drive Lyft and would be losing money. I planned a three-day trip to Cancun. Because he supposedly had no money, I told him I'd pay for the trip but that I wasn't going to be a sugar mama. He told me he would pay me back since it was my birthday trip, you know.

"I promise you I gotcha. I gotcha babe."

I was looking at it like that was something I should do to show that I was a good woman by his side. I was on the phone with Mickael while I looked at the different hotels. I texted him pictures to get his opinion. I booked a beautiful hotel suite, oceanside, with a balcony.

Mickael drove to Houston the night before we were going to fly to Cancun. The next day, when we got to the hotel, I was thrilled. We had a gorgeous ocean view, with a nice breeze blowing in across the sea. It made such a big difference. It was

69

nice and peaceful next to the ocean like that. We walked around the resort, got a few drinks, and went back to our room. We turned on some music and went out to sit on the balcony to talk. It was quite nice even though we were a bit tipsy from the drinks. We talked about our future together and how excited we were about being together and growing. As the perfect team, I was his life partner. Afterward, we enjoyed our exhibitionist show for the beachcombers below.

When we finished, we went back into the room. Mickael started cuddling with me, focused on me more than usual. I played on his arm and he wrapped it around me. He was so much more attentive. We cuddled the next day, too. We got up, had breakfast, and went out onto the beach. I had a little portable speaker, so we listened to music. A personal waiter came over, took our orders, and kept the drinks coming. It was real chill, like a great vibe, and I felt so much bonding. We went back to our room for more sex. A lot more sex. He was on top and looking into my eyes. We were so attuned to each other. It was amazing!

The next day was my birthday, so I was excited. Mickael woke up calling me bitch. Like something was up and I had no fucking clue what. I didn't cower. At all. I pushed back.

"You're calling me a bitch?! We've been in a relationship for over two years and you keep pulling this shit! Like I'm just some bitch off the street? And it's my fucking birthday!"

"Yeah, about that…I didn't have money to buy you a present."

"What? That's all I fucking asked for! Not even a two-dollar birthday card? You are fucking kidding me!"

His demeanor changed. Looking me in the eye, he said, "I'm sorry. Really, I'm sorry. And I didn't mean to call you a bitch. It just slipped out. Don't look at me like that baby."

I didn't say a word. I'm not the type of person who can hide my emotions. If I don't like someone, they're going to know I don't like them. I was way too pissed at Mickael for him not to know how pissed I was. Up until then, I'd been paying for everything on our trip: the flight, the hotel, food, drinks, tips, all of it. Suddenly, magically, Mickael comes up with some money and starts paying for shit. He became all accommodating. He knew how pissed I was all right.

That night we went to a strip club. There were all sorts of different people of different cultures. There was a great vibe. We enjoyed watching how they moved and the show the girls put on. Mickael bought us a bottle of tequila for the table. He asked me to pick out the chick I was the most attracted to. I told him which one I liked, so he paid for her to give me a lap dance.

The next morning, it was time to fly back. We took a taxi, and I cried and cried all the way to the airport. It was supposed to be a birthday celebration weekend. Instead, I paid for nearly everything. He couldn't get me a present. Not even a fucking card! It was like I was twelve again, sitting at the Red Lobster waiting for my mom to show up with a cake and a present.

I could see the taxi driver glancing at me in the rearview mirror – no doubt wondering why I was sobbing uncontrollably. I could tell he was concerned. He seemed more concerned than Mickael.

Not long after I started crying, I put on sunglasses so it would be less obvious just how big of a mess I was. I kept them on the rest of the cab ride and the entire flight back to Houston. We'd driven my car to the airport, so I drove us back to my place. Mickael said a quick goodbye and walked down around the corner to where he'd parked his car. It was gone. He found out it had been towed. He ran back to my place, then started yelling:

"My car got towed! You dumb ass! Why didn't you tell me not to park there?"

I didn't even know where he'd parked his fucking car. It was like it was my fault and I made him park there. Yeah, I made him come to Houston and get his car towed. It was all my fault. Like I made him go to Cancun, the trip I paid for. Like his car being towed somehow overshadowed the fact that he didn't even bother to get me anything for my birthday. Another prime example of how irrational he was and how he always made it sound like the bad stuff was my fault.

The blame game isn't much of a game. At least, not if you're the one getting blamed.

Fuck you!

Fuck you!

Fuck you!

Fuck you!

17

"STICK 'EM UP!"

Mickael would always tell me that I didn't own shit. Constantly reminding me that I didn't own much of anything. "And if you ain't got shit, you aren't worth shit!"

He owned several properties, including the house he lived in. I was renting a townhouse. That made all the difference in the world about a person's value, according to Mickael. It was like he made me feel less – that kind of thing. I wasn't good enough because I didn't own anything.

One time we got in a serious fight after I asked him about one of his side fucks and why he passed them off as friends or denied their existence altogether. He threw it back at me. I was just a crazy, jealous bitch who kept on seeing shit that wasn't there. Not only crazy, but seeing things.

I'd flown to New Orleans one time. Mickael said I should just fly back to Houston. I was feeling like he was right. He pretended like he was about to take me to the airport. I loaded all my stuff in the truck. Mickael drove me to some abandoned houses. He got out of the truck and just took off walking. I looked around to try and figure out where he was going. I had no idea what he was up to, but it had to be no good. I immediately grabbed my stuff because I had a feeling he was going to leave me stranded. I took off down the street after him. I stopped walking when I saw he was in the yard of one of the properties he owned.

I walked toward him. He was standing on the porch. I stopped on the front lawn. We just looked at each other. Then he yelled:

"You got mad at me for nothing, bitch! I did nothing wrong. I'm not fucking with you. It's all in your fucked-up imagination." When he said that, my heart dropped. We had signed a contract about being loyal, honest, committed to being together and supporting each other. None of this was in the contract.

I got so furious and filled with anger because I genuinely felt like I'd been played. The next thing I know, I balled up my fist and smacked him in his face. It caught him off guard. He had on a hoodie and stuck his hands in the big front pocket. I figured he was cold. Instead, he pulled out a gun and pointed it directly at my head. I looked him in the eye, and he looked all wild-eyed.

I surprised myself. My response was anger. I directly confronted him, "Nigga, are you serious? You going to shoot me? What the fuck are you thinking?"

I kept staring at him and saw that he caught himself and put the gun back in his pocket. He went behind the house and stashed the gun somewhere. He came back out front and acted like he had calmed down. He said I should get a hotel room by the airport so I could catch a flight the next day. That's what I did. He took me to a hotel and even paid for the room. I stayed there until the next morning, when I could get a flight out.

I decided to leave Mickael because he was dangerous – in so many ways. A gun? I was in shock at the time, when I was staring down the barrel. My immediate response was anger and a ridiculous certainty that he wouldn't pull the trigger. On my flight back to Houston, after I'd had some rest and time away from all the craziness, I realized he could very easily have shot me. I was through with HIS crazy shit.

I should have known he'd call me when I got home. He was sorry. So sorry. He didn't mean to hurt me. He wouldn't really shoot me. He was just pissed off (as if that was some kind of an excuse). He wanted me in his life and couldn't imagine it without me (like if he shot me and I was dead). He said it all as if he meant it. He sounded so tender. Of course he did. He knew he'd blown it, big time. Still, that was what I chose to believe. I mean, I didn't think I was choosing anything at the time. I decided that was really how he felt. I figured he kept his tender feelings covered up by all that anger.

I called up the image of when I first met him in South Carolina. I could see that look in his eye when he said the line: "When God puts somebody in your life, never take them for granted."

Why was it that line started all the trouble, and perpetuated it? It was seared into my heart. Like it was my cue from God. "Proof" God was in this with us. I just had to be patient while Mickael was working through his shit. I'm not sure why I thought he was working on anything besides doing whatever the fuck he felt like doing. I was so sure he wouldn't ever take me for granted (even though he already had), I was always holding onto that. I kept believing it, regardless of all the evidence to the contrary. His actions didn't ever seem to match what he was saying, and what I chose to believe.

Forget that Mickael was a compulsive liar. Looking back, I can see none of it was real, except for maybe pointing a gun at my head. That was real.

DEAR GOD, PART I

I love you.

I need you.

I thought you gave me Mickael,

Now I'm not so sure

I'm so crazy in love

I can't see straight

I need your perspective from above

Mickael has been wonderful to me

And horrible to me

I've given him money when he said he needed it

I've given him my heart when he said he wanted it

I've given him everything

With nothing in return

Loving Mickael has me hating myself

Please God, help me love Nya again

18

FROM STUPID IN LOVE
TO VENGEFUL IN HATE

I admit it. I have a temper. Now, in my defense, let me add that it takes a lot to send me over the edge. With Mickael, he made it easy to turn my love into hate. I suppose there's opposition to everything. Our love was passionate. So was our hate. There had been several intense altercations, but I got pushed too far. Or, shoved too far. I couldn't match his strength in a physical fight, but I was confident I could fight back in my own way.

One night on the phone, we had our worst fight ever. I could tell there was some other woman at his house, just by the way he was talking and how he didn't want me to go visit him the next day. I'd finally learned how to tell when he was lying and act on it. I hung up the phone and began to plot my revenge. I could contain my anger no longer. And since I couldn't contain it, I drove to New Orleans the next morning, fuming all the way down I-10. I knew he'd be at work. I had a key to his house, so I let myself in. I went upstairs, grabbed all his favorite clothes, threw them in the tub, and poured in straight bleach. The whole bottle. I glanced over at the nightstand and saw the top of an opened Magnum wrapper (and no, he hadn't used it with me).

I wrote him a note that simply said, "It's time to cut the cord." Then I grabbed scissors and proceeded to cut every single cord I could find: to his coffee maker, two TVs, a radio alarm clock, three extension cords, his Alexa ("Can you say, 'cut the cord' Alexa?"), the toaster, the microwave, and four lamps. It was like each time I cut a cord, I felt like I was cutting Mickael out of my life. It felt so good that I went into his closet and cut up the rest of his clothes.

As I drove out of sight, I sent Mickael a text that said, "I told you not to mess with me. I have finally cut the cord. Good-bye."

I knew he'd be furious. I expected an angry phone call or perhaps an angry visit. For whatever reason, I wasn't afraid of him coming over. I was prepared to call 911 if he came anywhere near me. And I'd be the one to call 911 this time. He'd be trespassing on *my* property. I was pretty sure the cops would take my side.

He was angry all right. But not so angry that he bothered to come to Houston. I'm sure he was more focused on his new piece of ass. Why ruin the mood? He called and started screaming at me. This time, rather than my anger escalating along with his, which is what usually happened, I became calmer and calmer. It was cathartic. It carried with it a deep sense of satisfaction. Like my hurt was overshadowed by his, for once. I'd never really been able to get to him like that before.

Good sense would dictate that would be the end. I was fed up. Overfed up. I felt a renewed strength and determination to be done. I should have known he'd call again.

And he did call, again.

And I did get back with him, again.

And again.

And again.

And again.

Loving Wrong

I never thought love could be wrong

Nothing in this world is more important

Love one another, as Jesus said

But now it's too late

I should have recognized the hatred in your eyes

Your really big bug eyes

And your really big hands

That can spread hate more easily than love

Your lies

Your anger

You and all your hoes

Your broken promises

Have become my broken promises, too

And then there's my broken heart

Have you ever heard of true love?

Or loyalty?

Or trust?

Yes, love can be wrong

You're proof of that

19

BIPOLAR? PTSD? SCHIZOPHRENIA? DEPRESSION? NARCISSISTIC? ALCOHOLIC? YES.

Mickael's mom was always warning him that his dad had serious mental health issues so he could very well end up with issues, too. I think Mickael used alcohol, addictively, because he was trying to escape his mental illness, like depression. That never works very well, especially since alcohol is a depressant. He checked into a rehab place for his alcoholism for thirty days while we were dating. They diagnosed him while he was in there, listing multiple mental health issues. I saw the paperwork when I picked him up after the 30 days. It listed PTSD, schizophrenia, anxiety and depression. After dating him for a while, I'd diagnosed the bipolar. I picked up on it because he could walk out of a room and come back a different person. He won't own up to any of his disorders.

Dr. Jekyll and Mr. Hyde. One day he could be so sweet, so loving, wanting us to work together and work it out. He'd start touching my skin: "I love the way your skin feels. I love the way all of you feels."

Then the flip side. The next day he'd say how he didn't care about me and didn't trust me. Suddenly, he'd start screaming at me. From one extreme to the next.

"Bitch, you aren't doing me right. This isn't fucking working."

He'd put on headphones, so he didn't have to listen to me and then he'd just pace from room to room. Crazy. Fucking crazy. I knew something wasn't right. But initially, he had me thinking it was me. That it had to be me who was doing crazy shit. He made me feel that way all the time.

Pick a mental illness. Any mental illness.

Unhinged

Unhinged.

Deranged.

Frenzied.

Unbalanced.

Manic.

Disturbed.

Mental.

Psychopath.

Lunatic.

Out of one's mind.

Control freak.

Wacked out.

Mentally ill.

Narcissistic.

Schizophrenic.

Bipolar.

Personality disordered.

A few fries short of a Happy Meal.

Two pills shy of sanity.

Mother fucker.

It describes my mother and my lover.

20

FRENCH QUARTERS

One time I was deployed to New Orleans for Hurricane Ida and got this great hotel room. I could stay wherever I wanted as long as it was within the per diem rate. So I chose to stay in the French Quarters, right off of Canal Street. Those were the best two months of my life, in part, because Mickael and I hardly fought at all.

He came and stayed with me there every weekend. One of those weekends, Mickael suggested we spice it up. So I googled clubs and found that there was a swingers' club just two blocks away from us. Mickael was like, "Okay, cool. Let's do it. We gotta make a list of dos and don'ts first." Again, that spoke to the idea that he had done this before with someone else. I wouldn't have even thought of a list of dos and don'ts. So we made a list. And the list only restricted me, of course. I couldn't look at another man or talk to another man. Didn't sound much like swinging. Only from his perspective. If there was something I was interested in doing, I had to ask for his permission. If I was interested in a woman, she had to meet his approval.

We took a shower and got dressed. I went through three different dresses, and he finally approved the one for me to wear. I put on the dress and the approved makeup. As we walked over, we talked about how fun it was going to be.

We were surprised that it looked like a dungeon. While walking in, we passed several dominatrixes. A lady asked for our ID. Since we weren't members, we had to pay $100 per person to get in.

"The bottom level is the club level and up top, you'll find the Playhouse." She smiled as she said it, sorta like the Cheshire Cat.

We started at the bottom so we could have a few drinks. Then we danced a little bit – maybe two or three songs. Most of the people around us seemed pretty damn drunk. Just a bunch of plastered people. There was a pole and a drunk girl was trying to dance on it. Easy to tell she wasn't a pro. Although most of the people were drunk or high, they were also really high energy.

Then we decided to go up to the Playhouse. We took the elevator up – a very small, cramped elevator for two. When the doors opened, we could hear moaning, heavy breathing and ass slapping. We went down the long hallway. To the right was something that looked like a small lounge. There were a bunch of black sofas lined up in a U shape. There was a room to the left that looked like a tall parlor. All the walls were wooden. It was bizarre-looking, but also cool. In there were four couches arranged in a square, set up so everyone could see everyone else and what was going down. We sat on one of the couches. There was this Hispanic couple across from us. The chick was giving her dude serious head. Then she hopped on and straddled him, and he started bouncing her up and down, real forcefully. He gets up, bends her over, and goes at it even harder. She floats on top and you can hear her liquid squirting out all over him. On another couch was a super skinny chick with a really big dude. Real skinny and real big! She was on him, working to get him hard. She went to her knees and started giving him head. Then she straddled him and worked at it even more. He still wasn't hard – not for a lack of trying. You could see the frustration in her eyes.

On another couch was a guy who was getting off with himself as he watched everything else that was going on. Mickael and I were just sitting on the couch we'd claimed while watching what was going on around us. It was a turn-on, for sure. So, we enjoyed the show, watching them for a while.

I started caressing Mickael, rubbing him on top of his pants. Then I unbuttoned his pants and started giving him head. The whole time I was deep-throating him and licking him like a lollipop, a real loud lollipop. After a while, we decided to stop. The room had slowed down as everybody had kind of dispersed. We got up and walked down the hall, a little black hall that took off to the left. There were three open rooms set up with people going at it. There was a sheer curtain hanging in each doorway. As we passed by, we could hear them moan and even feel the ground shaking. To the right, there was this other room. The whole wall was glass. We walked past and could see everything going on. It was like we were in a museum watching a moving diorama. There was a big round bed in the middle with three couples. Two were having sex, missionary style. Another couple was going at it doggy style. Mickael and I stood and watched them.

Then we went back downstairs to get another drink. We talked for a while, but it was really loud. Still, I liked the whole vibe of the place. Mickael started feeling it so he took me back upstairs. We went to the room with the big round bed. Only two couples were doing it, so there was space for another couple. He took off my dress and put me on all fours – doggy style. Then he stood up on the side of the bed and pumped and pumped and pumped. I started moaning, but the couple

89

next to us was moaning even louder. It felt like a competition. When they moaned, I moaned…it was so exciting, it aroused all of us.

We grabbed some more drinks after we were worn out. We walked back to the hotel, talking about how much fun we'd had. It helped us bond. Yep, it was something sexual. What else would we have in common?

CRAZY IS AS CRAZY DOES, PART I

I am well aware that even though Mickael was crazy, so was I. However, Mickael helped drive me there. I didn't realize I was hitching a ride until it was too late. And crazy is as crazy does. I know I have neglect and abandonment issues. I came by them honestly. They were hard-earned.

When my momma picked us up and moved us away from Daddy, it was like he abandoned me, too. (Later I understood that my mom was to blame for that one). We never knew when my mom was going to show up or blow us off. I can't count how many times she left me stranded. I have no idea why I waited for her, with great anticipation and expectations. I'd wait hours on end. Eventually, I did catch on and quit counting on my mom for a single thing.

I was learning the same thing about Mickael. One time I was on the phone with him, and he was being an especially large asshole. He was also being dismissive, saying he didn't care if we stayed together or not. It was like I was disposable. He couldn't care less about me. I felt like it was my mom standing me up again. I started sobbing.

Mickael ignored me, then said, with disgust, "You're a grown-up. Get over it. You're being childish with your dumb-ass shit!"

I yelled back, "Just leave me the fuck alone! Why do you keep coming back into my life? I'm done! I'm done with everything!"

I'm not sure exactly what I meant when I said, "I'm done with everything!" Mickael didn't know, either. I hung up the phone, and he tried calling back, several times. I didn't pick up. I was numb. I went downstairs, walked out into the garage, got into my car, started it up, turned the music on, and sat there hoping to breathe enough carbon monoxide to do myself in. I didn't want to be alive anymore. I'd had it.

Meanwhile, unbeknownst to me, Mickael called the Houston police department. I guess he could tell how poorly I was doing. He told them to do a wellness check on me because he thought I was suicidal. It's one of the few times that rat bastard knew, and cared about, what I was feeling.

I'm not sure how long I was sitting there in the car. I was startled to my senses when someone banged on the garage door. I opened it up to see three cop cars and a fire engine. Two of the officers talked to me for a while. I can't remember anything they said to me. I just remember they put me in their police car and drove me to the mental hospital.

The hospital was everything I feared it might be. People were walking around like zombies, no doubt doing the Thorazine shuffle. What were they going to inject me with? Was I next? Did I belong in there? Would I end up leaving worse off than when I went in?

Suddenly this guy walks up to me and says, in a very loud whisper with his hand up to his mouth: "I work for the FBI. I'm only in here because I'm investigating the hospital to report on all the things they're doing wrong. And there's a lot of 'em." If he was an FBI agent pretending to be a patient, he was doing an amazing job. He was spot on with the gown, the blank stare, and shuffling about like a zombie.

The more I looked around, the more convinced I became that I was in the wrong place. Oh sure. There was the incident of me in my idling car…. But I felt far worse off being in the hospital than I did when I was sitting in my car, listening to music and sucking down carbon monoxide.

I fully expected Nurse Ratched to come up from behind and stick a needle in my ass. I kept turning around until I got dizzy. I guess paranoia was kicking in. Finally, I was taken to a psychiatrist's office. I swear, it seems to me that all psychiatrists need to be seeing a psychiatrist. This guy was no exception. He had a bad combover that he kept "combing over" with his hand. It wasn't simply about keeping his hair in place. I could tell it was also a nervous habit. I thought, *This guy is going to tell me what's wrong with me? Afterward, do I get to say what I think is wrong with him?*

His final assessment was depression and anxiety. High anxiety. *Did I really need some crazy doctor to tell me something I already knew?*

They let me out the next day. What happened to the 72-hour hold? I figured they didn't have enough beds to keep me any longer. Even though I hated the place, I did know I needed to be somewhere so I couldn't hurt myself (or hurt Mickael, for that matter).

If they weren't going to help me there, I was going to have to help myself. Typically, I was fully capable of taking care of myself. But this crash and burn, I was in a different place altogether. I figured I needed to concentrate on keeping myself alive.

I've worked at a suicide hotline before – ironically enough. Three-quarters of the calls were from people who just wanted to talk. It was the other 25% we had to worry about. With the people who were seriously suicidal, we were taught to help them find a reason to live. Even if it was just one reason. Most frequently, it was a family member or a partner. I could certainly scratch the partner off my hope list since he'd triggered me in the first place. There was my son. Yes. My son. His father was usually absent in his life. I was his caretaker and I loved that job. I loved *him*. There was no way I could ever abandon him because I knew what a traumatic experience that could be. And since he'd turned fifteen, we were starting to become friends, too. Lemar was my life, my loved one. Not Mickael.

My friends and cousins told me how fucked up it was that I didn't end it with Mickael right then and there. I didn't end visits to the psychiatric hospital, either.

It was like I was just a fun girl, a friendly fuck, someone he wouldn't ever take seriously. Shit hurt so bad because he was being so disrespectful toward our relationship. I felt so dumb. Stupid in love.

Stupid in love

I might be dumb but I'm not stupid.

Well, maybe stupid in love

You say the other woman (or women?) mean nothing

You say I'm your everything

Yeah, everything

like a chump

and a sucker

and a fool

I see so much in you

So much that isn't there

It could be, though, I'm sure

With the right woman

And the right woman is me

I know I am

I know a lot

It's just that I'm stupid in love

DEAR DIARY, PART II

November 4, 2018

Had a long conversation with Mickael, started off wanting to make decisions about his future; he felt like he didn't fully know me. So I opened up about my past, telling him about past relationships and the trials and tribulations I've endured. He said that helped him feel more connected, somehow. We talked for eight hours.

November 5, 2018

Again, had a good conversation; he expressed how he felt I had let my guard down and it made him want to let his down as well. We had a good day.

November 6, 2018

He called, we talked, he wanted to express that he loved me! He didn't want me to feel like he wasn't in it. That made me feel special. I had been begging him to express his love for me.

November 8, 2018

He came to visit me, and we had a good time. No complaints. He seemed like he missed me, and I felt like he was expressing his love.

November 12, 2018

He was playing one of his fucked-up games that made me feel like he wanted me to be insecure with our relationship. I called twice and he didn't answer. When I called again, he answered. There was an echo. I kept asking where he was, and he wouldn't tell me. He hung up and so I called him ten more times. He didn't answer and then sent me a text saying he was busy. I expressed to him that his actions were making me feel insecure. He told me I was tripping and that it was always something with me.

November 13, 2018

We talked about the bullshit I was dealing with at work and the change that went into effect about me working until Dec. 20th. I wouldn't be home for my birthday. I told him I was sad and wanted to know how I was supposed to look past it. He said he'd been saving up money for our trip and asked what he was supposed to do now that I had to work. He said, "When the 14th comes, we'll see then." That shit made me cry. My birthday was on the 10th. I knew the only connection he had to the 14th was Juvi's birthday. I asked him why he kept doing the same shit. He told me I take things too far and I was tripping. Then he got off the phone because he said he was having chest pain.

November 14, 2018

Called to check on him, but the first couple of times he didn't answer. So I sent a text saying I was just checking in on him. He texted back saying he was in the hospital and needed me to send him $250 for the charges. I called him a couple more times, to see what was going on, and he didn't answer. When he finally called back, he had an attitude and answered me with short, one-word answers. I told him that I was feeling like an outsider, not feeling like we were a team, so I wasn't going to send any money. At least not until he could hold a decent conversation with me. My cousin, Muffin, and I tag-teamed and called all of the area hospitals. She called the ones on the East and I called the ones on the Westbank. None of them had him listed as a patient. I knew he was lying again.

March 9, 2019

Talked early this morning. Had a good conversation. We didn't talk again until 11:30 at night. He had an attitude, and who knows what his attitude was for. He said he was gonna let me do his hair (he was growing his wicks). I told him he made it sound like a privilege. He took that as if I didn't want to do it, and the argument began.

April 16, 2019

Made it back home from Mickael's place in New Orleans: Lord, I need help! I'm weak, the devil is making me feel like I just want to quit on life. I don't know how to love JUST myself and it hurts that I don't feel any love in return from Mickael. I want this relationship to work and it isn't. I want my son to be strong and focused. I don't know how to get that to sink in. Lord, I love you. I know you are my strength, but I am having problems with my faith, Lord. I need you NOW. I need a blessing, I need to hear you, I need you to guide me! I need you to show me my happy place within. Teach me how to let go. Teach me how to love myself. Teach me how to find peace within.

April 18, 2019

Lord give me strength. Lord allow me to see the power within myself. Lord stop this weakness. Allow me to move on if I'm not wanted or appreciated. Allow me to know if you have a plan for me. Allow me to know that if one door closes, you'll open another one. Lord, I know you see my heart and I intend to help make people happy and lighten their loads. I've done much to help Mickael – from small things like making sure he always had food to sending hundreds of dollars when he's in a bind. I have nothing to show for it. A simple conversation with Mickael blew up, and he said he didn't want me anymore because I'm not the same person. He seems so angry and unhappy with me. Lord, heal my heart. I'm just tired of trying to fix things by myself. Help me, Lord!

May 21, 2019

We talked several times throughout the day. We started talking about a condom I saw in his wallet, weeks prior. I asked why, because he and I did not use condoms. He gave some bullshit story about the condom being old and dried out. I don't know why I keep wanting to believe him.

May 24, 2019

Got to New Orleans late Saturday night. We had a good night. The next morning, he was distant again. I asked him to come and watch church with me. He told me to leave him alone. That hurt my feelings because I had only been in town for twelve hours and wanted to spend time with him. He went pacing around and then went into his room for a long time. He was acting weird all day.

The next morning, he woke me up and was happy. He told me Happy Anniversary and kissed me. We went to the grocery store and went back to the house and cooked. We had a good day.

May 26, 2019

We woke up, went to the thrift store, got ice cream, came back, and Mickael went to sleep. When he got up, I noticed all his calls and how he'd run out of the room to answer them. When I asked him about them, he gave me some bullshit about it being his homeboys and him just wanting to "shoot the shit" with them. Whenever the phone rang, my heart sank. I knew he was full of shit. So I just shut down and went into silent mode. He came over and asked me for my keys. I pointed to my purse.

"Don't you hear me talking to you? Open your fucking mouth!" I just looked at him and didn't say a word. He walked off and when he came back, he went to my purse, grabbed my keys, and unlocked my Jeep, saying he was going to the store. After he came back, he ignored anything I said to him. I took some meds and went to sleep.

May 28, 2019

I stayed in bed this morning until it was time to go. When I was leaving, I poured the washer fluid into the tank until it was full and put the rest of it on the porch so he could use it in the other vehicles. He went and got the bottle and threw it away. Just childish, ugly shit. I finally left and he didn't call or text the entire way home. I'm feeling like this nigga doesn't care about me. He just talks crazy to me and makes me feel like I'm always in the wrong. I feel like his love is bad for me and I'm wasting my time with him.

May 21, 2020

He is having one of his moods, and I don't know what I did or what happened to change things. I'm trying not to get my feelings hurt by his distance. He is so mean to me. He called me "stupid" just because I said I didn't want any food.

May 22, 2020

He is making me feel so unwelcome. He has an attitude, he's distant, and he's only under me if he wants sex. He put all kinds of passion marks on my neck and is being so mean, like he has so much to do and I'm just in his way. This doesn't feel like love. Why does my presence make him so upset? Why is he so unhappy with me? Lord, what is the lesson you're trying to teach me through this storm? I need your guidance. My heart is hurting.

May 23, 2020

I needed to go to the doctor because I wasn't feeling good, I was bleeding and my stomach hurt. I told Mickael I needed to go to the ER. That started an argument, him saying I was a problem. It was always something with me. He said I was always having some kind of issue. If I was in that much pain then go to the hospital. He kept saying stuff, like accusing me of being the devil and saying I'm just looking for attention. He said if I called 911 then I should just pack up my shit and leave with the ambulance.

May 24, 2020

More fighting. He was mean to me all day, telling me he didn't want to fuck with me because I was full of chaos and he had no peace with me. After arguing for a while, I gave him his peace and went outside and got on the phone. After a couple of minutes, he came out and told me to go get us something to eat. "I want Applebee's!"

When I got back to the house, I fixed him a plate. When he finished eating, I tried to talk to him, but he kept walking from room to room. I asked him to be still and have an adult conversation. He refused. I started following him from room to room asking, "What's wrong? What did I do?" He got mad, slammed me against the wall, and choked me with his right hand as he pulled my hair with his left. He yelled, "Leave Me The Fuck Alone!" Finally, he let me go and dropped me onto the floor. I started crying, then I had a panic attack. He just left me on the floor gasping for air.

21

MISCARRIAGES OF JUSTICE

I got pregnant three times with Mickael. I also had three miscarriages. The first one was a total surprise because I didn't even know I was pregnant. My stomach started hurting, real bad. I knew it wasn't menstrual cramps because the pain was more intense. I went to the ER where they ran some tests and determined I was pregnant and in the process of miscarrying. I called Mickael and he acted all concerned. And that was just it, he *acted* concerned, but it wasn't sincere. Like he was an actor trying to deliver his lines and not doing a very good job.

"Oh, I am so sorry." "Be sure to get some rest." "You take care of yourself, babe." "I'll talk to you in a bit."

But he didn't call back that day. So, I gave him a call later the next day. He was a total asshole. No acting that time. He was himself. True blue. True to he, himself, and no one else.

"You aren't outta bed yet? You're shitting me! Get out of bed and do something. Anything. You gotta do something with your life. How the fuck do you expect to get anywhere when you're just being lazy?!"

No compassion. No understanding. No nothing. Just verbal abuse.

When I found out about the next pregnancy, I was so excited! I called Mickael and told him. He wasn't excited. At all. He said, "Well, we'll just deal with it." I'm pretty sure he was talking about an abortion. I didn't ask because I didn't want to know. I wasn't about to get an abortion.

I think Mickael was relieved when I miscarried. I was at Red Lobster with my son and started having horrible cramping with some bleeding. Again, I knew it wasn't my period. I went to sleep with a heating pad. The pain was even worse the next morning, so I went to the hospital. The nurse had me pee in a cup. When I did, the fetus fell into it. I was horrified! When I called Mickael, he started telling me about how I needed to be healthier. He said I was getting old so my chances of getting pregnant and staying pregnant were getting slim. Just a few of the precious sentiments Mickael shared with me.

During the third pregnancy, I went to the hospital and they sent me to a specialist. They found that the fetus was in my right fallopian tube. They told me I needed to have the fetus removed right away. I didn't want to, so they had me sign a paper stating I knew I was in grave danger. (What else was new?) Mickael came down to Houston and came to the hospital.

Two days before Memorial Day, I went to New Orleans. Mickael and I had sex and he was very aggressive. Because he's so well-endowed, he was up in my stomach and all. I started bleeding and he still had sex with me. I began cramping and said I had to go to the ER.

In his kind way, he said, "It's always some shit with you!"

I was in so much pain, I started crying. "*Call an ambulance!*"

"I'm busy, you call an ambulance. I got shit to do, woman." He went outside to cut the grass. I waited for a bit and then told him I was going to call 911.

"Wait! Don't you call an ambulance! I don't want one coming to my house and drawing all that attention."

Which is why he finally agreed to take me. At the hospital, I was told I needed to go through surgery. I felt like they were taking something from me. I wanted more kids. They were going to take my tube and I'd get a shot that would dissolve my baby. They kept telling me I needed to be safe. I told them I was going to drive back to Houston. They said I'd be taking a huge risk. The whole thing was a huge risk. I kept choosing to ignore medical advice because I wanted that baby to live. It was *our* baby.

Despite what kept happening with Mickael, I still wanted to have a baby with him. The thought of getting a shot that would dissolve our baby was out of the question. Mickael couldn't understand why I was making such a big deal out of it.

I drove back to Houston and ended up in the hospital again. The pain was unbearable, so I had no choice. They performed the surgery and gave me the shot to dissolve "the fetus." It wasn't just some fetus. It was my child they would be dissolving, along with my hopes and dreams of who that child could grow up to be.

Mickael didn't care. He couldn't understand. He didn't have a dissolving baby inside of him.

A miscarriage of injustice

Three months is a long time to carry a child

It's more than enough time to form a bond

To grow attached

By then he has arms and legs

Fingers and toes

Most importantly, a heart

That beats with mine

And to rip him from me?

To dissolve him away?

It's like there's a death in the family

But there isn't a funeral

No flowers

No eulogy

No notes of consolation

Just solitary sorrow

Made that much more solitary

Because there's one less heart

Beating within

It's a miscarriage

A miscarriage of injustice

22

GOD'S TESTING ONE OF US

It was October 2019. Mickael and I had been in a good space for a few months. It was time for me to get my annual pap smear, so I scheduled an appointment with my OBGYN, Dr. Katz. He was familiar with my case as he was the same doctor who had taken care of me with all three of my miscarriages.

The doctor and I exchanged small talk before he began his examination. He called his nurse into the room and asked me to lay back, place both feet in the stirrups, and open wide. He inserted the speculum then stretched and stretched until he could see my uterus. He inserted the Q-tip, twirled it around, and pulled it out, giving it to the nurse to be tested. He told me to sit up since he was done with that portion of the exam.

Then it was time for him to do a breast exam. He started with my left breast, holding it in both of his hands and gently pressing around to see if he could detect any lumps. He finished with the left breast and said, "Feels fine to me." Then he walked to my right side to perform the same test. However, when he held my right breast in his hands and started pressing around, he got extremely quiet for several minutes. He broke the silence with, "Put your hand where mine is. I want you to feel this." As I did he said, "Do you feel that lump?"

I managed to utter "yes" although I felt like my heart was in my throat. He told me that it was abnormal, and he needed to refer me to a specialist, a breast cancer specialist, who worked at the MD Anderson Cancer Center. That was one of the best hospitals for cancer patients in the southern region. My heart dropped and I felt even more fear. Breast cancer didn't run in my family. "How could I have it?"

I left the doctor's office in mental anguish. I started crying and immediately called Mickael. I couldn't get the words out of my mouth to explain what had just happened. I could only blurt out, "I need you."

He asked what was wrong. I told him I'd call him when I got home. I couldn't stop crying long enough to tell him at that moment. I drove home talking to God the whole way. "Lord why me? Who is going to take care of me? Who is going to raise my son?"

After I got home, I called Mickael back. When he answered, he said, "Now tell me what's wrong."

I held back my tears and said, "They found a lump in my breast, and I have to go see a specialist." I was afraid it would trigger memories of his wife's death from cancer. But I should have known better.

"Oh, is that all? I thought there was really something wrong with you!" I told him I was scared. He fired back, "Why are you scared? Millions of women are told they have lumps in their breasts. You're no different than they are!"

He told me to stop crying because he didn't feel like dealing with all my "emotional shit." We got off the phone and I cried myself to sleep – because of the lump, and because of Mickael.

The next day, I had to call the specialist to schedule an appointment. I couldn't be seen until the following week.

During that time, Mickael and I didn't speak much. The few times we did, he criticized me for being so emotional. He'd say things like, "Nadia went through all the doctors' visits and testing by herself because I was working overseas."

Everything I was going through got compared to what Nadia went through when she was diagnosed with breast cancer. He acted like he knew everything I was feeling because he saw how Nadia reacted (forget that he was overseas most of the time). He figured he'd lived it before, so he was now the Guru of Breast Cancer.

When it was finally time for my appointment with the specialist, Mickael was still being an asshole. I had been venting to my cousin, Muffin. She was my strength. The morning of my appointment, she called to pray with me, asking the Lord to give me strength, to cover me with his blood, to protect me, to heal me.

Soon after I got there, a nurse called my name to come on back. When I got to the room, she handed me a gown and said, "The doctor will be in shortly." I sat there for about 15 minutes waiting, my mind racing, my heart beating fast.

The doctor finally entered. She was nice, extremely compassionate, and seemed to genuinely care. She explained the process and was open to any questions I had. She examined my right breast and said, "Yes, that's definitely a lump."

Tears started running down my cheek. "So what do I have to do next?"

"I am going to schedule you for a mammogram."

The soonest mammogram appointment I could get was another week away. During the waiting, I tried to talk to Mickael in hopes of getting some support. No such luck. He had no compassion for what I was going through. All of my pain, my worries, and my concerns kept falling on deaf ears. And a cold heart. I couldn't understand why he wouldn't just be supportive of me. Yes, Nadia died from breast cancer, but I was alive and begging for his support. He wouldn't have it.

The morning of my mammogram appointment, I was an emotional wreck. I was scared as hell. The American Cancer Society recommends women start getting breast exams at age 40. I was only 37. I sat in the waiting room with dark sunglasses on, hoping it would hide the tears that kept running down my face.

I chanted over and over… "So do not fear, for I am with you; do not be dismayed, for I am your God. I will strengthen you and help you; I will uphold you with my righteous right hand (Isaiah 41:10)."

Also, "I can do all things through him who gives me strength (Philippians 4:13)."

Minutes later, the nurse called my name to come on back. When I sat down, she gave me an overview of the procedure and told me what to expect. Then she gave me a gown to change into.

As she walked away, she said, "Just a minute. A technician will be in shortly." I changed into the gown and just sat there staring at the walls, with high anticipation. The technician walked in and asked me to go over to the machine. She guided me through how to properly place each breast in the mammogram machine. The machine pressed down, surprisingly hard, as she snapped images. It was painful. Imagine your breast being flattened like a pancake, for several minutes. The technician finished the exam, told me to get dressed, and explained that it would take a few days to get the results.

As I waited, yet again, this time to hear the life or death verdict, I was even more of an emotional wreck. Mickael wasn't communicating with me much. When he did, he kept scolding me for being so emotional.

"Nadia didn't do this crybaby shit you're doing. Remember, she went to all her doctor appointments alone. She was strong. Why are you so weak? Grow the hell up! There's nothing wrong with you!"

I couldn't understand, for the life of me, why he wouldn't want to support me. It was baffling.

If you lose one woman you loved to breast cancer, why wouldn't you be there for the woman you currently love who has a lump in her breast? What happened to "When God puts someone in your life, never take them for granted?"

A few days later, the doctor called with the results of the mammogram. Indeed, there was a large mass in my right breast. She said to schedule a biopsy. The first available appointment was ten days later (just my luck). During that waiting period, I became severely depressed. I felt alone like I was supposed to have a man, a partner, someone who loved me and assured me everything would be okay.

One night as I cried myself to sleep, I had an epiphany. This was a test from God, but who was he testing? For me to have this scare and for it to be drawn out over time, causing my emotions to run wild, was anomalous. A few days later it hit me. This was Mickael's test from God. Would he be supportive? Would he show empathy and compassion? Or, would he be the same nonchalant asshole with me as he was with Nadia? Would he take another woman for granted, just like he said he'd never do again? The answers were blatantly obvious. I stopped all communication with him.

Finally, the anxiously awaited day arrived – my biopsy appointment. I was surprised at how much pain the biopsy caused. I had to use an ice pack for the next few days. Then came even more anxious waiting – for the results.

The news came shortly before my birthday, on December 6th. It was benign. Happy birthday indeed!

I was so grateful and found myself wanting to tell Mickael, even though I could imagine him saying something like, "See, you made a big deal out of nothing." Regardless, I couldn't quite let go. I prayed to God and told him how grateful I was that I'd been spared from cancer. Then I took it one step further. Knowing I really shouldn't ask God for a sign, I asked for one anyway. I told God that if I was supposed to stay with Mickael, if he was the one, then please have him come visit me. The next day, at 9:00 in the morning, there was a knock at the door. It was Mickael.

In hindsight, I realize the devil can hear our prayers, too.

DEAR GOD, PART II

I need help!

I am spent!

My mind is willing

But my flesh is weak

So is my heart

I love him

Even though I finally know you didn't put us together

Please, help tear us apart

All that's being torn apart right now

Is my heart

I know you are my strength

Because I have none

I don't want to go on

I can't go on

Without you

Without you I am nothing

Please, speak up

I can't hear you

Are you there?

Somewhere?

Anywhere?

You say have faith

But right now my faith is blind

I can't see you

I don't expect absolute proof

I don't expect your full attention

Just a nod in my direction will do

23

LIKE FATHER,
NOT ALWAYS LIKE SON

When I met Mickael's son, Amaro , I was surprised. I thought he'd be like Mickael – cocky, arrogant, and a ladies' man. He was fourteen at the time, and very timid. You got the feeling he was walking on eggshells and like he was working to keep everything in line. He washed the dishes like they were all fine china. At first, I was dumbfounded, then curious, and then it hit me. Of course, Amaro felt like he was walking on eggshells. I felt that same way around Mickael, too. There was no telling how he was going to act from one minute to the next. He's probably beaten the shit out of Amaro, plenty of times.

I learned Mickael's discipline could be severe, and bizarre. He had this man cave, which was an extra room attached to the back of the house – like a build-out. The walls were made of wood, the top was covered with metal, and the windows were made with mesh screens. There was a door that opened up to the backyard. Inside the man cave was a little portable fireplace. There were two recliner chairs, a chaise lounge, and a TV and radio. Oh, and yes, there was a bar.

Amaro came home with a poor grade one time. As punishment, Mickael made him sleep in the man cave for three nights. That wouldn't have been so bad except it was December and freezing outside. There wasn't a heater, just the portable fireplace, which wasn't helpful. And, Mickael locked him out of the house. That was his punishment.

When Amaro turned sixteen, Mickael took him out to "turn him into a real man." (As if Mickael had any idea what a real man was.) He put him in the car and took him to the hood. First, he found a kid selling weed on the street corner. He bought some and made Amaro smoke it. Amaro wasn't into that sort of thing. He did a lot of coughing while Mickael called him a pussy.

"C'mon, smoke some more! You didn't get shit in you yet. Breathe deep!"

Then he flagged down a hooker and gave her twenty bucks. "Hey, give my son here some good head. It might even be his first time. Amaro, is this your first time?" He refused to respond.

"Okay, c'mon. Pull your dick out and show her what you're working with!" He unzipped Amaro's pants and pulled his dick out.

Talking to the hooker again he said, "See, check out the size of his dick. Is he a man or what?" Yes, that was Mickael's idea of a man. He was very proud of how well-endowed he was. Very narcissistic-like.

Giving in, knowing refusal would be fruitless, Amaro got out of the car and walked over to the prostitute. She knelt down and started sucking on his dick. Mickael felt the need to cheer them on. He started hooting as he beat on his chest like King Kong.

"Fuck yeah boy! You go!"

I know about it because Mickael was so proud of their adventure, he told me all about it, sparing no detail.

When Amaro went to college, he went to Northwestern University in Louisiana because Mickael kept pushing him there. Mickael had been to the campus several times when Nadia went there so he was familiar with it. Sometimes he could be a chicken – a coward – and seek after the familiar because the unknown frightened him. Forget what would have been best for his son. Mickael is such an egotistical, selfish son of a bitch.

After Amaro went to college, he never looked back. He never called home again. He never answered Mickael's calls. He never went home during breaks. If fact, he never even called to ask for a single dime. It was obvious he wanted nothing to do with his dad. Oh, and he majored in psychology. He'd had plenty of on-the-job training growing up.

Mickael spun the whole situation to make himself look good. Again.

"I hardly ever hear from Amaro because he's so busy with school and homework. And he has a job now, too, because it's important to him to earn his way through school. I'm proud of him because I raised him to be a man (oh, right). He's out on his own and all independent."

Bullshit. Amaro just didn't want to be beholden to him. He didn't want to have anything to do with the bastard. He only went home for funerals.

It was a pity I couldn't be as strong as Amaro.

The pros and the cons

Pros

Independent

Motivator

Ambitious

Business savvy

Great chemistry/sex

We have fun together (yes, I wrote that in the present tense)

Similar interests

Did I mention great sex?

Cons

Cheater

Asshole

Dismissive

Selfish

Deadbeat to two of his kids

Physically and verbally abusive

Disrespectful

A liar

Unsupportive

Coward

Poor communication skills

Inconsistent

In denial about his mental illnesses

Confused about religion

Certain he is never wrong

Unwilling to change

Unwilling to learn my love language

There are twice as many cons as there are pros. However, I must confess that the "Great chemistry" and "We have fun together" count for about ten points each. Plenty of people will read those lists and think I was crazy for dating him and staying with him. Others know precisely what it's like. You may try to break up but the harder you try, the harder it gets to leave. Men like Mickael know how to work it. They know how to turn up the charm when they think you're ready to walk out. Either they pour on the charm or escalate the abuse, putting you "in your place" and making it so you feel powerless.

I've never had anyone make me feel powerless before. I've never cowered in the corner feeling unable to go anywhere. Why do women stay with men like that? I'm pretty sure it's impossible to explain to someone who hasn't been in such a relationship. That is due, in part, to the fact that it defies logic. It's that logic and such strong emotions don't mix. It's like one or the other, and emotions usually prevail.

Pros? I was crazy in love. Cons? I was crazy in love.

CRAZY IS AS CRAZY DOES, PART II

It was several months after my first breakdown. I was in New Orleans for a week and a half, visiting Mickael. Things had improved and were going well. We were lovey-dovey and all, bonding and spending quality time together.

Suddenly, Mickael switched over to Mr. Hyde.

"Why the fuck are you even here? I'm not feeling it!" By the way, we were naked, and I was laying on his chest as he spoke. "I don't feel it!"

I was shocked (yes, he could still do things that shocked me). This was some crazy shit for sure. I stood up, put on my clothes, and asked "What's wrong with you? What just happened?"

"I said, I don't feel it"

I would have left right then but it was pouring rain, the kind of rain that happens in New Orleans when windshield wipers can't work fast enough to keep the windshield clean, even on the highest setting. I remember thinking how fitting it was to have such a night with pouring rain, inside and out.

I went into the other bedroom, closed the door, and tried to get some sleep. I just laid there and listened to the rain pounding down and wondered why I kept taking all his shit. My depression started pouring down on me, too. I wanted, so badly, for the rain to stop so I could get the hell out of there.

Suddenly Mickael grabbed the door and threw it open. I looked up and said, "I'm tired. Why do you keep doing me like this?"

"Boo-hoo. Are you going to start crying again? Listen, babe, if you're going to kill yourself, then go ahead and do it." He was dead serious.

So, I ran to the kitchen, grabbed a butcher knife, and began cutting away at my wrist. I was numb and just kept slicing. I wasn't looking for attention. I was looking for death. I'd had it with life.

Mickael grabbed the knife from me and held my arms down as he called 911. Soon the cops showed up and hauled me off to the mental hospital. It was a similar experience to before, but this time I was in a New Orleans hospital rather than a Houston one.

There was a backdoor in the place that seemed to lead to another unit or something. Whenever staff would open the door, at least one of the patients would dash to the door and try to get through it. This kept happening. It seemed like there had to be a better system of moving about. I couldn't figure out why so many patients were trying to run through the door. It seemed to me like the other side of the door was just more of the same.

One dude said he was Big Chucky and his friend, Little Chucky, was waiting for him at home. That freaked me out because I hated the movie *Child's Play*. I mean, hated it! The man wasn't dressed like the doll, but just the thought of that guy, a very big guy, calling himself Big Chucky was creepy enough. I knew suicide was a threat, but did I belong in this place? Does it help people feel better when they see a bunch of people who are worse off than they are? What are the stats on that anyway?

As I was imagining a doll's attack, I asked the nurse if it was time for my evaluation. She said, quite gruffly, "They aren't ready for you yet. Go sit down!" (I had found Nurse Ratched.) I thought she was going to drug me. I refused to sit and was ready for a fight.

Maybe she recognized the look in my eye. She called over three coworkers who were nearby, watching TV in the dayroom. They pushed me to the floor and dragged me to a room where they strapped me down, both wrists and both ankles, and gave me a shot to "settle me down."

After two or three hours, a doctor came in to diagnose me – with depression and anxiety. (I could have told him that.) Again, they let me go so I needed to pull myself out of it. Mickael picked me up but was very pissed off. As usual, he blamed me. Again, it was all my fault.

After we got to his place, I went in and took a shower. Alone. Mickael never asked how I was doing or even made a single comment about what had happened.

And no, that wasn't the end of it. Crazy is as crazy does. Part I, Part II, and beyond. My love ran deeper than the cuts on my wrist.

We Wish You a Merry Christmas

We Wish You a Merry Christmas
We Wish You a Merry Christmas
And a Happy New Life

24

HOME FOR THE HOLIDAYS?

My son hated Mickael. He didn't tell me until last Christmas, but I should have figured it out long before that.

It began with another December birthday trip. My birthday is exactly two weeks before Christmas, and it was my 40th birthday. This time we went on a cruise and Mickael actually paid for it. We swam with the dolphins, took an art gallery tour on the ship, and hung out on a beach in Mexico. For my birthday evening, we attended the captain's ball. They gave me a small cake that said, "Happy Birthday" and a bunch of people sang to me.

After the cruise, we each returned to our homes (Mickael drove from Houston to New Orleans since he didn't get his car towed). No sooner did he arrive than we talked on the phone. He started up with his attitude again. As usual, I had no idea why, or what had happened. No doubt it was my fault. Still, I asked what was wrong.

"Why does there always have to be something wrong, nosy bitch?"

I was wondering the same thing. I asked, "What's on your mind? What's going on inside your head?"

He yelled back at me, "I told you, nothing!" It sure didn't sound like nothing.

He quieted down and was actually decent. Then I could tell he just drifted off. While he did his drifting, I was like, "Fuck it." I think it was also something about turning forty that woke me up.

As I hung up the phone, I thought "I'm not gonna keep dealing with this bullshit. If you don't want me, you don't want me. And I don't want someone who doesn't want me. I don't want to keep going through this shit into my forties. I want to get married and settle down with someone who truly loves me and wants me. Who wants to be a partner. A steady partner. Someone who treats me well."

So I didn't call him. I'd had it.

A few days before Christmas, he started calling me again. He was fairly nice and even said he wanted to spend Christmas with me. He never wanted to do that before.

"So what are we gonna plan? What are we gonna do for Christmas?"

"How about we go to Orange Beach, Alabama?"

I don't know why he was so big on Gulf Shores, Alabama, and Orange Beach. He was always wanting to see those places. He came up with a plan that my son and I would drive down to New Orleans. Then, with him and two of his kids, we'd all go together to Gulf Shores. He kept going back and forth with the plans, never solidifying anything. Fortunately, I waited to tell my son because it was highly likely that Mickael would pull out entirely. I knew he'd finally made the decision when he booked an Airbnb in Gulf Shores. I was so excited that we were going to spend Christmas together.

I went into my son's room to tell him. It was his freshman year at Grambling State University, and he was home on winter break. I guess I shouldn't have been surprised. I told him to get his stuff together and pack a bag because we were going away for Christmas, meeting up with Mickael and his two kids.

"Mom, I don't want to go. I want to stay home for Christmas, and I don't want to go anywhere with Mickael." I was shocked by his answer, for some crazy reason. But I was all excited about the trip. I went in there thinking he'd be excited, too.

I asked him again to pack his bag so we could hit the road.

"He's an asshole and he doesn't give a fuck about you, Mom. Not a fuck! He treats you like shit! I've never seen you more miserable than when you're with Mickael." From the mouths of babes, like my 18-year-old son.

I'd normally beat the shit out of him if he talked to me the way he did. I think, deep inside, I understood. And he definitely explained himself, in case I didn't know.

I had to reflect on everything Lemar had seen growing up. Everything he knew had taken place. He knew that I was in a psych ward twice. When I locked myself in the garage and the police were knocking on the garage door, he was upstairs. He knew I went to jail that day in New Orleans because he couldn't find me for two days. My phone was off, and that was unusual because we talked every day, three times a day. He was scared to death. And he'd heard me in the next room, howling and screaming and crying while talking to Mickael. He saw me super depressed and didn't know what was wrong with me – at first. I didn't know what was wrong with me, either. Why I was so depressed. I would just pick him up from school in the afternoon and have something already fixed for dinner. I would lay in my bed by five o'clock and just stay in bed the rest of the night. I didn't come out of my room or talk to him. I stayed in my room on the weekends, too.

I hadn't ever gone into detail with Lemar about me and Mickael – about all the really bad shit. I didn't have to. He already hated everything about Mickael. I called Mickael and told him Lemar didn't want to go. I didn't tell him what Lemar said though. That was all I needed.

"He just doesn't want to go."

"Well then fuck it. Let's cancel the trip."

"I can still go. I want to go."

"I don't feel comfortable with it being just me, you, and my kids."

"What's the difference if Lemar doesn't come? We can still be like a family."

"Too late now. It's been canceled." I knew that was bullshit because we were still on the phone talking about canceling the trip and he didn't have time to cancel anything. Fucker. He is such a control freak! It was always his way or the highway.

Gee, I don't know why my son doesn't like him.

25

CONTROLLING ME, AND
THE NARRATIVE

Mickael had been violent one too many times. I finally filed a restraining order. Later he told me he decided to forgive me for filing the order – as if I were the one who had to be forgiven. He was putting the control back in his hands.

"All you need to do is pay me back for the lawyers I had to pay when you filed charges, bitch. It was over $4000. And, get two tattoos to prove your devotion to me. Then take a picture every day with a different affirmation written on your body for me."

"What the fuck?"

"If you aren't willing to make up for what you did by filing a restraining order against me, I can't imagine us fucking around anymore." He hung up, keeping control of the whole narrative, yet again.

Later he sent me a message saying he could only text me on WhatsApp because the judge put an app on his phone to track his communications with me, until the court date. I asked if they had a warrant. He said yes. I didn't believe him, so I told him to send me a screenshot of it. He claimed the image wouldn't upload so he couldn't send the picture. Instead, he sent a link from the internet and said, "It's like the one in the middle." He was lying his ass off.

A few days later, he sent a message saying he wanted to extend an olive branch and come for the weekend since it was Valentine's day weekend, so he could show me how much he loved me. We chatted for a while, planning for him to come out. The next day he sent a message saying he had bought an airline ticket. The plan was for us to hang out for the Super Bowl in Cincinnati since the Bengals were playing, then drive back to Lexington, Kentucky so I could work on Monday. When I got off work, we could go to dinner and then he would leave on Tuesday.

The next morning he sent me a message saying that his momma had an episode (referring to her having nightmares and sleepwalking). He had to take her to the ER so he couldn't make his flight. He apologized, saying he knew I felt our relationship was on the back burner, but some things weren't "in his control." Right. Everything was in his control and if it wasn't, he knew how to make it that way. I guess he felt guilty; he sent me $300 as a Valentine's Day gift.

The more I thought about it all, the more I knew he was lying. I was sure he hadn't planned to come to see me in the first place. It was just his way of fucking with me and "getting me back" for filing the restraining order. Emotionally, there was no real way to restrain him. Not physically, either.

He hates me, he hates me not, he hates me

He hates me not, he hates me, he hates me not
I hate him, I hate him not, I hate him
There's no room for love anymore
Just the fleeting absence of hate
And the absence of hate
Is a poor excuse for love

26

SIGNS FROM GOD.
AT LEAST, I HOPED SO.

Great chemistry is tough to find. Mickael is the only person I've ever had that much chemistry with. Looking back on how I thought we were brought together by God, I think I'd have to call it "hormonal revelation." I was sure all that chemistry was a sign. I was sure of that because Mickael said, "When God puts someone in your life, don't take them for granted." I thought that meant God was putting him in my life. And I shouldn't take him for granted.

Why didn't God tell me I was way off base? Why didn't he help me? I used to wonder that. However, I'm realizing that God could have been shouting at me to "Get the hell out of that relationship!" And even if he was, I couldn't have heard the message over the chemistry. It's amazing how "distracting" great sex can be. More than once, I used the ridiculous line, "If it feels this good then it must be right." Like the ol' "If it feels good, do it." That mantra isn't very helpful. There are a lot of things that feel good but are really bad ideas.

Staying with Mickael, for instance. At some point, the "feels good" shit got drowned out by the "feels like shit" shit. Talk about learning things the hard way....

Chemistry

A bond formed by love and hate

elation and devastation

ecstasy and agony

and ecstasy and ecstasy

It's chemistry

a covalent bond

sharing electrons

attracted to each other's nuclei

love on the subatomic level

27

FORGIVE ME

Please forgive me for being weak. Forgive me for not remembering that my strength comes from you. For not asking you for it when I needed it. Forgive me for loving a man more than I love you or myself. Forgive me for doubting myself, for hating myself. Forgive me for allowing myself to be abused. I need you, Lord. I've held onto Mickael for so long because I thought you sent him to me. Sincerely, in my heart, I believed you brought him to me because I had been praying for a companion. I had been begging you to send someone with a like-mind who I could grow with. I thought I met him. The way things seemed to come together, I believed you sent him. I wanted to do everything differently so I wouldn't lose him. I didn't want to be selfish; I didn't want to be shallow or put myself on a pedestal. He didn't have the things that I was used to having in a man like a nice car and money to spend, even if just on special occasions. I overlooked all that, thinking that is what a good woman does. I feel as though a trick has been played on me, like I've been made a fool of. I *have* been made a fool of, but it's Mickael who made me the fool, not you.

DEAR GOD, PART III

You threw everything at me

I took it, but I didn't take it well

I walked through the valley of the shadow of death

And I feared no evil

I should have feared evil

I should have recognized evil in Mickael's eyes

I spent so much time and energy seeking after him

I forgot to seek after Thee

I want to repent

Not just forgiveness of my sins (and there are many)

Also, the repentance that changes human hearts

Instead of a stony heart with Mickael

Give me a "new heart" and a "new spirit"

"Take away the stony heart"

And give me a "heart of flesh"

Put your "spirit within" me (Ezek. 36:26)

You are the one in whom I shall trust

"How great is thy lovingkindness, O God!

therefore the children of men put their trust

under the shadow of thy wings (Psalm 36:7)."

28

THE STRAW THAT FINALLY BROKE THE CAMEL'S BACK

Why didn't I break up with him? I can't say how many times I asked myself that question. Friends and family asked me that question far more times than I asked myself. Unfortunately, I never really listened. After all, they didn't know how "wonderful" he could be. And, I'm not counting all the times I broke up with him, only to fall for his, "I'm sorry. I'll do you right. I love you."

It's like Mark Twain said, "Giving up smoking is the easiest thing in the world. I've done it a thousand times." I probably broke up with Mickael a thousand times. I lost track.

What made me break up with him for good? It was sorta more of the same. Too much of the same, I suppose. Same shit, different day, only worse shit than the average.

We ended up going to Orange Beach, Alabama in January. On the sixth day of our trip, his mom called and told him his nephew had died. He was in a bad car wreck at four o'clock that morning. He wasn't drunk. He was with some friends and they were driving too fast. They were trying to get home in time because he had to go to work. The car skidded off the road and hit a tree.

"Hey baby, I'm sorry, I'm so sorry. I got you. I'm right here."

He got up and started running all around the room. Then he went from one room to the next, howling the whole time. I start following him around, rubbing on his back.

"It's all right, baby. Calm down. It's okay."

He calmed down enough for me to get him in the car. I drove over to his mom's and his sister's.

"I love you. Be strong. Sorry I have to go. I have deployment orders. Just call whenever you need me. I can come back here whenever you want. Let me know when the funeral is, and I'll be there. I'm just gonna put a dress and heels in my suitcase. Whenever the service is, I can fly out and come with you."

I ended up going to Kentucky for work. The service was planned for the following week. It was going to be Martin Luther King weekend, so I figured I could fly out Friday because the funeral was set for Saturday. I called Mickael as I was getting ready to book the flight.

"No, don't book it!"

"What? Why not?"

"I don't feel comfortable with you around my family at a time like this. You know, I just don't feel comfortable."

"What do you mean? What the hell do you mean? I was there for you when you first heard about it. I saw how it affected you."

"I'm good. I'm good. I don't need anybody to console me. I'm good."

"What?! I saw you rolling all over the floor, crying. Why wouldn't I be there for you?"

"I'm good. I gotta take care of my people, you know."

His people? I wasn't his people, really? And he didn't even want me to be around them? That was a slap in the face. He knew he hurt me because I started to cry.

"I'm sorry. I knew it would be painful before I said it to you. I said to myself, 'Mickael, you 'bout to hurt this girl.'"

He did it anyway. He did it any fucking way. He knew how bad it was gonna hurt me and he still did it. He said I should just be supportive from a distance (whatever that meant).

That was the straw that broke the camel's back. I couldn't wrap my head around it. If I was his woman, weren't we supposed to be looking at a future together? Weren't we supposed to be there for each other? The guy who died wasn't just a nephew. He was like a brother to Mickael. Why wouldn't I be there? It made no sense. We'd been off and on since 2016. It had been almost six years.

After the funeral, my eyes were finally opened. Wide open. I started noticing his behavior, and his behavior had changed. He wouldn't do whatever he said he was going to do. Like call or call back. I'd call and wouldn't hear back from him till the next day. He'd ignore my texts completely. He wasn't being accountable for anything. I soon got tired of it and called him out on it. I started to have an attitude toward him. Started bitching about it and putting it in his face.

"Mickael, you've asked me to change and I've changed. I've been working hard at this relationship and you haven't done shit."

"Oh sure, fucking change. I know how women are. Sometimes I call in the evening and you're at the gym or on the treadmill. And you always talk about being on a diet. All of a sudden you want to eat right and shit. I know. That's what women do when they're trying to find a new man!"

"What the fuck? Because I'm trying to eat better and get in shape, you think I'm fucking someone else? You're fucking crazy. I hate to tell you, but you don't know women like you think you do! You're such an asshole!"

He hung up and didn't call back. I called days later, and he wouldn't return my calls. Any of them. I wondered how the hell he could be with somebody for so long and then just throw them off to the side like they're dirt.

Time went on. He still didn't call.

Then I quit calling.

He wasn't even man enough to break up with me. He wasn't even man enough for much of anything.

I'm woke

I was thrown in jail once (by the hand of my
boyfriend)
Beaten too many times to count (at the hand of my
abuser)
Screamed at and belittled constantly (from the mouth
of my lover)
A suicide scare, twice
The psyche ward, twice
Mental health issues, off and on
I loved a hater
While holding onto a dream
That was really a nightmare
But now I'm woke
Resiliency
Perseverance
Patience
Waiting for the right man
Who could be right around the corner
I know this much
He won't be an abuser, or a liar, or a narcissist, or a
cheater, or a mother fucker
Been there, done that
Now I'm woke

29

BONUS CHAPTER
WHEN COMMON SENSE ISN'T
SO COMMON

In 2004, a video was released showing Baltimore Ravens running back Ray Rice hitting his fiancée, Janay Palmer. He hit her so hard that he knocked her unconscious. Just one month later, Ray and Janay got married. The incident and the marriage that followed sparked a social media frenzy. The most popular post on Twitter was by Beverly Gooden: #WhyIStayed. In just under two days, it had been used 100,000 times. Later, the hashtag #WhyILeft also became popular. Countless stories were added from women, and some men, who had managed to escape abusive relationships and how they went about it. Wish I'd paid more attention. Little did I know how much I would need that information in the coming years.

I have learned a great deal through all of this. Part of the reason I've written this book is to help others in the same predicament I was in. Perhaps it's easier to see the mistakes of others and then apply them to our own lives. In addition, below I am sharing reasons women stay in abusive relationships, advice for gaining emotional sobriety, and tips on how to get out of abusive relationships. I believe knowledge is power. The power to reclaim lives, one woman at a time.

*Eight Reasons Women Stay in Abusive Relationships"

"1. Distorted Thoughts." Domestic violence is traumatic and that can make it difficult to think rationally. So can being in love with an abusive partner. Women are not at fault, even when, or especially when, an abuser tries to make them feel that way. People might say, "I believed I deserved it," and, "I was ashamed, embarrassed, and blamed myself because I thought I triggered him." Not true.

"2. Damaged Self-Worth." Part of not thinking clearly is the result of the physical and emotional damage done by the perpetrator. The self-worth is damaged, too. The relationship is degrading and defeating. Some women say things like, "He made me believe I was worthless and alone," and, "I felt I had done something wrong and I deserved it." Again, not true.

"3. Fear." There are many verbal and physical threats, and actions, hurled by the abuser. The fear can be crippling. There is a saying in therapy concerning the trauma response. People either "fight, flight or freeze." Women can feel paralyzed, and unable to move. Or, fight against the attacker, only to be beaten up even more.

"4. Wanting to be a Savior." The perpetrator can seem like a wounded man. Actually, he is the one doing the wounding.

151

Women often feel the need to try and save their partners. Like, he just hasn't been with the right woman yet and I'm the right woman. That is a myth.

"5. Children." So often women put their children first. The problem involved when there is an abuser in the house is that the children witness their mother being beaten or screamed at and/or suffer abuse themselves. Some mothers consider it important for the children to live with their father in the house. That isn't so if it's an abusive father. The opposite is true.

"6. Family Expectations and Experiences." Divorce can seem like a failure and not everyone understands. Others might expect you to "work it out." A good way to look at it is the fear of divorce can outweigh all the other negative things going on. One woman said, "My mother told me God would disown me if I broke up my marriage." God doesn't want anyone to stay in an abusive marriage.

"7. Financial Constraints." Abuse directly affects women, physically and emotionally, making it more difficult to get a job. It can also make it hard to keep a job. And, there's the threat of debt. As one woman said, "[My] ex racked up thousands of dollars of debt in my name." Not acceptable.

"8. Isolation." Frequently an abuser will isolate his partner, so she is out of contact with family and friends. He often feels threatened by any outside influence because he wants complete control, all the while showing no self-control.

Women can be perpetrators, too, although that is less common. The same tips generally apply in these cases.

*(8 Reasons by Jason Whiting. Retrieved from:

https://ifstudies.org/blog/eight-reasons-women-stay-in-abusive-relationships)

Gaining Emotional Sobriety

Emotional sobriety is tough to define and acquire. It involves being aware of your emotions and allowing yourself to experience them. It's important to know when to explore feelings and when to remain calm or indifferent so you can process them later when it's safe.

S – Silence. Take a break from the chaos. Enjoy times of solitude and meditation.

O – Observe don't absorb. Be aware of what is going on and just observe. Keep the immediate, destructive emotions at bay.

B – Breathe, breathe, breathe. Deep abdominal breathing, using the diaphragm, helps reduce stress. It also gives you time to consider what you want to do or feel next.

R – Remain non-reactive. An angry response is likely to trigger another angry response from the perpetrator. Instead of reacting, try to calmly think of how you want to respond.

I – Ignore. Not every rude, mean, or abusive attack needs to be answered. Ignore what is being said in anger.

E – Establish no contact. Keep yourself physically separate from the abusive partner whenever possible, even if it means going to a women's shelter.

T – Total indifference. Developing an attitude of indifference makes it more difficult for an explosive partner to continue exploding. There's no engagement.

Y – You can be authentically happy with your life. You deserve it, even if your abusive partner has you thinking that you don't.

"Kindness without honesty equals manipulation"

Dr. Les Carter

*How to Leave an Abusive Relationship

Step 1: Prepare yourself emotionally

To gather the strength to leave, it's important to have "all your wits about you," so to speak. Seek help if need be so you can view yourself, your partner, and your situation more accurately.

"Give words to your experience"

By talking to others you trust, you can get honest and fairly objective feedback. Giving honest input is important, too. In that way, others can help give you a clearer view of your predicament and how to get out of it.

"Keep a journal"

Not only is it helpful to talk to others, but it's also important to write down your feelings in a journal. That can help you get feelings out, work through them, and view your situation more clearly. Just be sure to write in a safe, secure place and keep your journal hidden.

"Realize your partner won't change"

That is such an important realization. Often women feel they can change their partner. Like he just needs the right woman to do the job properly. Change can be difficult and it's nearly impossible when someone doesn't want to change. Just because an abuser may promise change, and even does so for a short time, he seldom sustains it.

"Be ready to grieve"

It's a loss. A huge loss. Most women are bound the strongest by love. That can outweigh everything else. You need time to grieve the loss and even the thought of the loss.

"Step 2: Lay the groundwork"

It's best to plan how you are going to move out and where you'll be moving to.

"Don't telegraph your plans"

Only tell a few people you're planning to leave. You want to make sure it doesn't get back to your partner. Be careful with your own emotions while you're around him, too. You don't want to blurt out that you're going to get a restraining order or leave in the heat of the moment.

"Erase your digital footprint"

Perpetrators want control and often want to know everything a partner is doing. It isn't hard to discover what you've been searching for on your phone or the internet. That's why it's important to go to a library or a friend's house to use a computer privately and safely.

"Pack your bags"

You'll want to gather all your important information like birth certificates, a marriage certificate, bank cards, and things like that. Store this information in a safe place, in case you haven't already.

"Enlist professional allies"

If you can afford a therapist and/or a lawyer, they can be a great help. Some specialize in domestic violence and have specific experience. Professional advice can be better than family's or friends' advice because it is more objective and backed by more experience. Especially when kids are involved, you'll want professional advice from a family lawyer.

"Figure out where you'll go"

Avoid any of the obvious places your partner would look, like at your parents' house or that of a good friend. If you don't know of anyone to move in with, you can also go to a domestic violence shelter.

"Be alert to your partner's changes in behavior"

You may notice an increase or a decrease in violent behavior. Sometimes this signifies the abuser is trying to manipulate you into staying – either by making you fearful or trying to get you to love him more.

"Have a code word"

For added safety, you can give family and/or friends a certain code word that stands for danger, please come over or call for help.

"ID a secure room"

Look around your house to find the room or rooms that would be the safest for you to hide in and lock. Be sure to take your phone with you so you can call for help.

"Step 3: Get out fast"

"Pick a safe time, not necessarily the 'right time'"

It may not ever feel like the right time to leave because you have so many conflicting emotions. Don't base your decision to leave on your emotions. Instead, plan to leave when it's safe. When he's gone to work or out with friends.

"Step 4: Once you're out of the house"

"Keep your whereabouts secret"

You don't want him to find you so don't broadcast where you're going.

"File the restraining order"

Have a lawyer file a restraining order or you can do it yourself. Remember that it's only temporary, and you can get a permanent one with a family court judge.

"Stop all contact with your partner"

Staying away, for good, takes a lot of restraint. Again, the loss is great. The loss is real, even though the relationship was destructive. Saying goodbye to it, once and for all, can also be empowering.

"Don't leave clues"

There's no need to change your address ahead of time. You run the risk of having your partner discover it. That includes your driver's license and forwarded mail.

"Be prepared to call 911"

Your life, and your children's lives, could very well be at stake. If possible, call 911 from a separate room, your safe room. If you fear he'll be dangerously upset with you because of it, remember it's important. And that's the perfect time to leave him. For good.

*(How to Leave an Abusive Relationship by Linda Rodgers. Retrieved from

https://www.thehealthy.com/family/relationships/how-to-leave-an-abusive-relationship/

En masse

Me too

You too

Us

We

Strength in numbers

Empowerment en masse

Reach out

Take the hand of another

On the same road

United we stand

Undivided we rise

Above the oppression

The abuse

The ugliness

Where beauty awaits

Stand up and see

ABOUT THE AUTHOR

Nya Kumari was born and raised in Houston, Texas. She was raised by a single father where she developed ambition and a determination to succeed. Her high school years and graduation took place at Jesse H. Jones High School in South Park, one of Houston's hoods. She went on to attend HBCU Wiley College, majoring in Criminal Justice and went home to graduate from HBCU Texas Southern University with her Bachelor's degree in Criminal

Justice minoring in Communication. She also collected a Merit Award, the Dean's List, and Honor Roll. Her proudest accomplishment is giving birth to her son, Lemar, and raising him as a single mother. She worked vigorously to keep a roof

over their heads and food on the table. Her vast array of jobs and work experience include: the City of Houston, the State of Texas, and the Federal Government, bartending, teaching adults English as a second language, substitute teaching, driving Uber, and delivering Grubhub – sometimes working three jobs at a time. Her life was turned upside down when she fell in love with the wrong person. Despite that traumatic, volatile relationship, she is still a hopeless romantic, believing in love at first sight and finding a soul mate.

A true story based on the author's personal experience, ***THE MIND GAMES HE PLAYED*** is Nya Kumari's first published book.